TRUMPED

TRUMPED

THE NEW AMERICAN REVOLUTION

BY J.B. WILLIAMS & TIMOTHY HARRINGTON

Charters of Freedom Publishers, LLC. Cheyenne, WY 82001

Library of Congress-in-Publication Data
J.B. Williams & Timothy Harrington
TRUMPED: The New American Revolution
Charters of Freedom Publishers, LLC
1107 West Sixth Avenue
Cheyenne, Wyoming 82001

www.COFBooks.com

Printed in the United States of America by
Thomson-Shore Co., Dexter, Michigan

The publisher is not responsible for web sites (or their content)
that are not owned by the publisher.

Front cover image: Shutterstock.com
Back cover graphic: Maria Williams

ISBN 978-0-9976301-0-7
1. Journalism — Political aspects — United States
2. United States Politics and Government 2016
3. History — United States
Send all inquiries to publisher,
Charters of Freedom Publishers, LLC
1107 West Sixth Avenue, Suite B
Cheyenne, Wyoming 82001

The story behind TRUMPED: The New American Revolution began in June 2015 when Donald Trump decided to answer the call to high public office. It is still unfolding today and will continue to unfold for weeks, months and years to come. TRUMPED is about *the rise of the silent majority* and their clear intent to reclaim their land, resetting the course of their nation and re-establishing firm foundations for the future of freedom and liberty.

First and foremost, we dedicate this book to the true foundation of freedom and liberty, our *Creator,* who endowed every American with certain *inalienable rights* and has guided our lives and our nation for many years.

Second, to our families who have sacrificed so much for so many years, as we served the cause of freedom and liberty, both in and out of uniform, and continue to serve today through the many works that led us to this moment. Without their unwavering love, encouragement and support, nothing would be possible or worthy.

Next, to *the people* who believed in us over many years, once strangers, now family, Daniel and Linda Garcia; Col. James and Barbara Harding, USAF (Ret.); Richard Van Waes; Barbara Ketay; Stephen Pidgeon, J.D.; Twana Blevins; Col. Harry Riley, US Army (Ret.); Robert A. Davis, USAF (Ret.); Shane Christiansen; Cris Smith; Maureen Mead; Vicki Webster; Karen Bracken; David Vance, US Army, (Ret.); Ed Anthony, US Army (Ret.) and all veterans and active duty members of the United States Armed Services. Special thanks to the United States Marine Corps and all members of The United States Patriots Union, Veteran Defenders of America, The Constitutional Accountability Coalition and all who support The North American Law Center.

Last, but not least, to all who are responsible for the peaceful uprising that is the subject of TRUMPED: The New American Revolution, wherein *the people* are uniting in an effort to retake control of the once conservative Republican Party and the United States of America, without whom, there would be no story. We dedicate this book to a brighter American future, when we will once again be one nation, under God, indivisible, with liberty and justice for all.

Thank you all!

J.B. Williams
Timothy Harrington

Contents

TRUMPED

PREFACE

For many years in America, *the people* had been growing increasingly discontented with the political class in both major political parties. As the nation entered the 2016 election cycle, the public approval rating of both political parties in Washington, D.C. had reached an all-time low, with public approval of Congress at or below 11%, indicating that approximately 90% of the population, regardless of past political affiliations, was dissatisfied with a government supposed to be of, by and for the people. Faith in the judicial branch was even worse and the Obama administration had transformed what was supposed to be the least powerful branch of the federal government into an unbridled tyrannical dictatorship, seemingly free from any constitutional checks and balances.

Not only was Washington, D.C. known for its paralysis, its perpetual partisan gridlock wherein nothing positive seemed to ever get accomplished in the halls of government anymore, but what little was getting done, seemed to be entirely anti-American and at odds with the vast majority of Americans.

The voting demographics of the country, as well as the level of disinformation, poor education and a steady diet of media propaganda, had changed the country dramatically over the past 50 years or so, but especially over the past 25. The mantra of the 2008 Obama campaign was "Hope and Change" and the notion that the Obama movement was going to "fundamentally transform America." But how and into what?

TRUMPED is a story that answers many of these questions. It's also a story about how the people would in the end react to their country being "fundamentally transformed" right before their eyes and how this would shape events unfolding in the 2016 elections. A sea change was taking place and almost no one in Washington, D.C. saw it coming or had any idea just how powerful this Trump tsunami was. It was about to hit the political establishment with gale force at a time when they believed the average American no longer cared and was willing to quietly go along with just about anything.

On the Democratic Party side of the country, discontent with status quo candidates like Hillary and Bill Clinton, or even Joe Biden, was materializing in the highly unlikely success of the Bernie Sanders campaign. Sanders had been a far-left fringe member of Congress since assuming office as a U.S. Senator from Vermont in January 2007. Beyond his rantings about free stuff for everyone, his political career was entirely void of any accomplishments. Yet, compared to Hillary Clinton, who along with her husband Bill, had a long and distinguished resume full of criminal activities, Bernie seemed the lesser of two evils to many traditional Democrat voters, especially young voters who had lost all hope for a bright future.

As the Sanders campaign was threatening to burn the DNC Convention to the ground in an effort to move the Democratic Party even further to the political left, a quiet coup was underway over on the Republican side of the aisle as well.

The 2016 U.S. presidential election would be the year of the political outsiders — anyone who did not come from inside the D.C. Beltway establishment. It would also be the year of the political phenomenon that manifest in both the Sanders and the Trump campaigns — one built by youthful voters who only saw hope in a Marxist future of collectivism and the other built by people behind American entrepreneur and self-made billionaire Donald Trump, who still believe in American exceptionalism. The election cycle would confuse, confound and even frighten both political parties, the nation and much of the world. For those of us old enough to remember, it was a very Reaganesque moment in history from the start.

Despite heavy insider advantages for Hillary Clinton, she would be unable to stop the growing movement behind Sanders from derailing what she assumed would be a walk-in-the-park to the White House. Just as she was unexpectedly derailed by Obama in the 2008 DNC primaries, Sanders was causing her fits in 2016.

Across the aisle, by midway through the spring nomination primaries, the nation was shifting further and further towards Trump. Republicans, Independents and Democrats alike would soon come to understand that the *Trump phenomenon* was about much more than one candidate, one party, one race, one religion, one partisan ideology or any one issue. Even Trump himself would struggle to understand exactly what was happening in a rapidly growing take-no-prisoners revolution in his name.

A separate book could be written about Sanders and Clinton. This book will focus on the growing movement to *TRUMP* the nation in 2016: The New American Revolution, which many hope will be the 2016 turning point for America.

According to his Republican challengers, Democrat opponents and the party-controlled U.S. media, this was all about a man who had made his name a household word after decades of building a high-profile enterprise, including hit television shows, all of which bear the name Trump. Everyone would soon come to understand that the man was nearly incidental to a national uprising now unfolding under that same name. They were being TRUMPED!

To be sure, Donald Trump will go down in history with the credit for striking the match. But the powder keg and fuse were already there, and inside the Beltway politicians on both sides of the aisle had been pouring gasoline all over the country for years. Whoever showed up willing to strike the first match would immediately become the organic leader of a revolution that even its leader would have to rush to understand.

In the 240 years since America declared its independence from England and established a republican form of self-governance under the Constitution of the United States, this country has faced many enemies of freedom and liberty. After gaining sovereignty in the American Revolution (1775 – 1783), the fledgling nation went on to fight the Barbary Wars and the War of 1812 (1801 – 1815), the Mexican-American War (1846 – 1848), the U.S. Civil War (1861 – 1865) and the Spanish-American War of 1898.

We survived World War I (1914 – 1918), World War II

(1939 – 1945), the Korean War (1950 – 1953) and the Vietnam War (1960 – 1975) as well as Gulf War I (1990) and II (2003), which followed the worst act of aggression against the United States since Pearl Harbor, on September 11, 2001. Since its inception, America has had to be forever vigilant and ready to defend itself against the enemies of freedom and liberty.

After all the blood that was spilled and lives that were sacrificed in battle against external enemies, we would soon find our nation under attack from internal forces. Donald Trump would find himself the unexpected leader of an organic revolution to save our Constitutional republic from enemies within. Maybe Trump always knew this day would come. Maybe he didn't. Maybe he, like most Americans, assumed the government would at some point self-correct. Maybe he thought funding and/or voting for the right politicians would turn the country around at some point, without having to directly take the bull by the horns.

No matter what he thought prior to the 2016 election cycle, nothing that had happened in our first 240-year history would prepare the American people — or Donald Trump — for the fight they were about to enter in 2016. This time, the nation was at war from within — but not, as in the Civil War (the war of northern aggression over central vs. state powers) between brother and brother or father and son. This war pitted the people against the government they had allowed to assume destructive levels of power.

Trump would find himself at the epicenter of the battle for the future of the United States of America. The enemy was an American cabal of political, educational and legal minds that had set their sights on destroying the republic almost 50 years ago when they wrote their counter-revolution manifesto based upon failed communist leaders from all over the globe and hundreds of years of history. Their stated purpose was to destroy what they had deemed an "evil imperialist empire" of criminal capitalists. Who better to lead the new revolution against the global communist counter-revolution than one of America's most famous capitalist success stories, Donald Trump?

If you're starting to think this is a political endorsement book for the Trump campaign, think again. The Trump campaign has had nothing to do with the writing, editing or publishing of this book. Furthermore, we are not in the business of endorsing any political candidates, ever. In fact, no one in the Trump campaign even knows this book is being written, and they may or may not like it once it's finished.

This book is our effort to share with the American people and freedom-loving people throughout the world, the true nature of American exceptionalism, the uniquely American spirit of true freedom and liberty. We are presenting the facts about how a group of anti-American communist zealots almost succeeded in destroying the United States, and how the American people—not Donald Trump alone — would save the republic.

This book is being written because, while most Americans can tell that something is very wrong in this country today, they do not know how this happened. They don't know who is responsible for our current plight, or how what they are doing right now in the name of a Trump for President campaign may indeed save their beloved nation from certain destruction.

Most likely, Trump himself will learn things about his own campaign for the presidency, and possibly his own future admin-istration as well, that he would not know without reading this book. Very few people in America have spent the past 25 years researching every facet of the global left's effort to take over and destroy the United States of America — and what can be done to stop it. However, the information provided in this book is based upon more than 25 years of in-depth research on these matters, representing only the tip of the iceberg overall, as this book focuses only upon the 2016 elections.

The aim of this book is to share with the American people the real truth behind the Trump phenomenon, The New American Revolution, *the rise of the silent majority.* This book is intended to help the people reclaim control of their political parties and their country.

This book is about the anti-American counter-revolution to destroy this country, and the rising second American Revolution to save it. This book is titled TRUMPED, but it is really about the people and the movement behind Trump. We will expose the enemy within, and the unlikely heroes soon to be. We will expose those who have demonstrated their hatred, disdain and ill will for all American principles, values and people, as well as those who are standing in the gap, for and with the American people.

On a cold blustery Veterans Day in 2011, we stood on the Washington Mall and proclaimed our intentions to reclaim and restore our Constitutional Republic. On that day, a dear friend Ed Anthony, uttered these words:

> *"This nation was not built by extraordinary men doing ordinary things. It was built by ordinary men and women, doing extraordinary things."* — Ed Anthony, Washington, D.C. Mall on November 11, 2011

Ed was right! And nothing has really changed since then. Today, in 2016, once again some very ordinary American men and women will do some very extraordinary things, all in the name of freedom and liberty.

In writing this book, we ask for the divine blessings of Almighty God to guide our hearts and our hands as we write these words. We pray that we can present them in such a manner that will allow all who read these pages to know the truth, and all who know the truth to rise together in defense of freedom and liberty and the rule of Constitutional law, and to reclaim the land which was endowed by our Creator, and so richly blessed.

This book is about how one man at the front of one movement TRUMPED an entire cabal of evildoers who thought they had the end of the United States within their grasp. It's about how millions of ordinary men and women made it possible for that one man to rise above even his own ambitions, answering a call to greatness beyond his imagination.

This book is about the land of the free and home of the brave. It's about AMERICA!

The Trump phenomenon isn't about Donald Trump. It's about the American people vs. the Washington, D.C. establishment which has undermined our Constitution and Bill of Rights for over a century now. It's about D.C. "experts" and political elites who have driven our nation to more than $20 trillion in debt and another one hundred-twenty trillion in unfunded liabilities, thereby threatening the U.S. dollar and everything Americans have toiled and sacrificed to build for generations.

The Trump revolution is all about all the king's men, vs. Trump and the American people, the American way of life and the future of freedom and liberty the world over. This is not really about Trump — but it sure is about time for *the silent majority* to make this stand.

The deliberations of the Constitutional Convention of 1787 were held in strict secrecy. Consequently, anxious citizens gathered outside Independence Hall when the proceedings ended in order to learn what had been produced behind closed doors. The answer was provided immediately. A Mrs. Powel of Philadelphia asked Benjamin Franklin, "Well, Doctor, what have we got, a republic or a monarchy?" With no hesitation whatsoever, Franklin responded, "A republic, if you can keep it."

What Happened to Our Country?

CHAPTER I

Time passes so quickly and everything on earth is in a constant state of change, most of that change, so gradual that we barely notice just how fast or how much things are changing right under our noses.

When we happen to notice changes occurring, we often assume that those changes are happening naturally, organically, just part of the evolution of mankind and shifting political views. Seldom does the average person look close enough at those changes to notice that almost every political shift is happening under the political agenda of someone. Almost nothing in the political arena happens organically. In fact, almost nothing is ever even left to chance.

So many questions, so few answers, none of which make any sense to the average onlooker.

In a nation born of Christian principles and values, still populated by a people, over 70% of whom are Christians, how did our country become so anti-Christian? When did the American people lose all reverence for the sanctity and value of human life? Why do we have so little regard for the gift of life that we allow over a million innocent, defenseless American infants to be aborted every year, and then ask why the American youth has such little regard for human life that they gun each other down on the streets or in a high school classroom?

Why do illegal migrants and Middle Eastern "refugees" (potential terror sleeper cells) in our country seem to have more "constitutional rights" than any legal American citizen? When collectivism in all of its forms, Marxism, socialism, communism, totalitarianism, fascism, Maoism, liberalism and progressivism has enjoyed a 100% failure rate all over the globe, why are so many of America's young clinging to the concept of central power and collectivism?

Why does it not matter which political party is in power? Why does the nation remain on a collision course no matter the outcome of any election in the past 30-years or so? Why don't 50% of legal Americans vote? Why are millions of illegal aliens and even dead people allowed to vote?

With all that taxpayers spend on government controlled education, allegedly to improve the quality of substandard education in a nation slipping behind the world academically, why is our society becoming less and less educated and more and more indoctrinated by the day? With the trillions we have spent over the past hundred years to "make everyone socio-economically equal" in America, why are we not equal yet? After decades of effort to eliminate racism in America, how are we more divided by race today than at any time since the Civil War?

Is it all an organic accident? Or is it all someone's agenda?

As you read these pages, you will begin to see a pattern develop, which will confirm that none of these things are accidental, natural or organic. All of it was indeed, someone's agenda. All of it is happening with intent and purpose. Someone is responsible for all of it. At the end of the day, the American people are responsible for allowing it to happen and allowing it to continue.

In any democratic system of self-governance, in this case, a constitutional republic, the buck stops with *the people*. At all times, *the people* have the government they allow to exist, either through action or inaction. If government is bad, it is our fault. If government is good, it is to our own credit.

To be sure, *the powers that be* use all tools of the trade to control *the people* and force them to carry out the will of the political ruling class. They control almost all the weapons of political warfare. To control a society, you need only control public sentiments. To control public sentiments, you need only control the flow and content of public information.

To control the flow and content of public information in the information age, you must control government talking points, academia and education, the news media, the entertainment industry, all social media and monitor private communications. You must control the dialogue. If you do not control the public dialogue and create *public opinion*, you cannot control society. You can only control the government by controlling *the people*.

The United States was not designed to be a nation of socio-economic, ethnic, racial, religious and partisan political voting blocs. It was designed to be a free nation of rugged self-reliant, self-governed individuals, each of whom would be free and able to determine his own station in life and place in the world based upon the size of his individual dreams and value of his individual efforts.

But today, many Americans see themselves as mere members of one voting bloc or another, based on race, economic status, religious beliefs or family voting traditions. They no longer see themselves as individuals who are free or able to determine their own destiny. Even though they see others strive and achieve greatness, they somehow believe that greatness is out of reach for them — that the dream belongs to someone else. To get their "fair share," they must rely on someone to confiscate from those who have and redistribute to those without.

Yet, the people make no connection between their efforts to vote themselves *equality through central collective power* and Marxism, the concept of "from each according to his ability; to each according to his need," despite the obvious direct connection.

Today, Marxism is so popular in America that openly avowed Socialist Bernie Sanders is giving closet Marxist Hillary Clinton a very real run for her money in the DNC primaries. Supporters of both are being "community organized" to violently protest and riot against Republican Party nominee and well-known "capitalist pig" Donald Trump, a self-made billionaire with a resume full of personal executive achievements.

If you think this is all organic or accidental, you are not thinking at all. Everything that has happened in the United States over the past 240 years has happened as a result of someone's agenda. All of it has happened by design. Everything happening today is on one side, the result of a counter-revolution against America that has existed for more than a hundred years and on the other side, a public uprising against it in the form of a new American

Revolution to reinstate and reinforce the rule of constitutional law.

In short, there is a current effort to overthrow the Democratic Party by those who believe that party is not yet socialist enough. This group is represented by Vermont Senator Bernie Sanders and they are giving the DNC establishment fits, threatening not only the crowning of Hillary Clinton as queen of the Democratic Party, but the future viability of the party itself.

Across the aisle, the Trump revolution has already seized control of the Republican Party via the GOP primary process. The people behind the Trump revolution are driven by the reality that the Republican Party has become indistinguishable from the Democratic Party at the national level, rendering the U.S. Congress almost obsolete as a representative body of, by and for the people and a constitutional check and balance intended to limit the power of the other two federal branches to their constitutional authority.

Despite unprecedented efforts by GOP elites to block *the Trump train* via all previously successful primary manipulation tools, the people simply overwhelmed the GOP machine at the polls in a quiet coup d'état that hoisted D.C. outsider Trump to political power over a party that had become a mere extension of the Democratic Party in recent years.

Whereas the Sanders revolt inside the DNC was an effort to force the Democratic Party and nation even further to the left, the Trump revolution was an overt effort to force the GOP and the nation to take a hard right turn in order to walk the nation back from the brink of extinction.

In both cases, what was happening in the 2016 election cycle was an act of desperation on the part of voters. In the case of the Sanders revolt, people promised socio-economic equality via federal confiscation and redistribution of other people's wealth had never realized the benefits promised over many years of wealth confiscation and redistribution. Democrat voters were becoming increasingly aware of the fact that the political ruling class was the only beneficiary of decades of federal confiscation of private assets and now, their earnings and assets were being targeted as well.

As the cost of a college education was being driven out of reach for any average American student and student debts skyrocketed, opportunities for employment after college were shrinking to a point when 90% of college graduates were unable to find work in their degreed professions. The promises made to numerous generations were not kept, for the young or the old. The so-called "party of the middle class" was now openly targeting the middle class until there would be no middle class left in America.

Despite claims of 5.5% unemployment rates associated with only those still eligible to draw unemployment benefits, the real rate of unemployment in the United States was pushing above 10% with another estimated 30% under-employed — working jobs below their training and education level for less money than they expected while they pursued their college degrees, digging a student debt hole.

In reality, the true economic condition of the United States is worse than that of the Great Depression. Following the stock market crash of 1929, unemployment reached the 30% mark. But it was much more visible then as people stood in government bread and soup lines in order to feed their families. Today those lines are invisible, with 40% of Americans receiving some form and level of financial aid from the federal government under numerous social service programs intended to keep the real economic calamity far from public view via Electronic Benefits Transfer (EBT) cards in place of soup lines. No wonder 40% of American adults are also on some form of anti-depressant.

Still, the people were feeling the pinch at home as their dollars bought less and less and each dollar was noticeably harder to come by. Despite all establishment efforts to paint Trump a "rude loud-mouth, bombastic, capitalist pig," Trump was drawing support from across all past political lines of division. For the first time ever, even labor unions were shifting away from the Democrat candidates towards Trump. Why? Because, even labor unions were being forced into extinction by their past Democratic friends who had driven nearly every manufacturing industry overseas, leaving millions of union workers unemployed or under-employed and on federal benefits to keep their families fed. No candidate on the Democratic side of the election had ever employed anyone, or met a payroll before entering politics. But Trump employed thousands, including union laborers over many years, before entering politics.

When Democrats talked for decades about creating jobs, they were talking about growing government and creating more government jobs. But when Trump talked about job creation, he was talking about real private sector jobs, gainful employment, something every American wants and needs regardless of past partisan leanings.

What had happened to our country was allowed to happen by *the people*. Our country was being driven into a *New World Order* which threatened our very existence. By the time *the people* started to take notice that their country was in deep peril, they would struggle to figure out how to regain control and save their country for themselves.

As *the people* started searching for ways to regain control, they would go through a process of relearning the control mechanisms put in place by our Founders 240 years ago. They would also learn that many of those control mechanisms had been altered or eliminated by way of precedence setting in their own governmental *rule making, executive orders and court decisions.* They would attempt to use all original checks and balance of power mechanisms, each step of the process, learning that the establishment powers had incrementally erected road blocks to all of those checks and balances over many years.

As *the people* eliminated option after option in their efforts to regain control, they would find themselves forced to relearn the fundamentals of self-governance in a constitutional republic in order to regain control through peaceful political processes. Despite unprecedented efforts by party elites, the establishment would not be able to control or overcome that *uprising* in the end.

Eventually, *the people* would relearn that "all politics is local."

All Politics Is Local

CHAPTER II

For far too many Americans, Ronald Reagan represents the last time they voted for a presidential candidate, as opposed to only voting *against* a candidate and for "the lesser of two evils." That was 36 years ago, in 1980, when Reagan, like Trump, was able to win the American vote, crossing all political partisan lines after narrowly winning the GOP nomination.

It is not too much to say that the great bulk of citizens, the country over, are in a state of ignorance about politics. Their ideas about political organizations are of the haziest nature. The general belief about a political machine is that it is a sinister and somewhat secret association of men who run politics, live by graft and are headed by bosses who come up from the slums and are exceedingly evil creatures. Of the real functions of the machine, of the kind of men who belong to it, what they do, how they do it, what they get out of it, great political power is acquired, how and why it is held, there is an amazing lack of accurate information. There is a slight conception of either the necessity or the importance of the machine and the vital nature of the primaries, if we can judge by the absurdly small percentage of voters who regularly participate in them, is generally missed. – Frank R. Kent, 1923 [1]

Frank Richardson Kent (1877 – 1958) was a highly regarded political journalist during the 1920s and 30s. Although he was a lifelong Democrat, he was also the leading ultra-conservative critic of Roosevelt's New Deal. Kent was one of the big-name journalists who covered the Scopes "Monkey Trial" in 1925 and although once revered by FDR, who even helped Kent to become a syndicated columnist based in Baltimore, Kent became FDR's and the new American left's biggest critic. Despite being a lifelong Democrat, Kent cherished classic liberal Jeffersonian principles as opposed to today's leftist progressive

Frank Richardson Kent, April 1928. [2]

principles far from Jefferson's ideals: a balanced budget, limited spending by the federal government and a limited government in general. His growing criticisms of the new Democrats grew ever more severe throughout his journalistic career. Kent rightly charged that the Democrats no longer stood for state's or individual rights and that was almost a hundred years ago now.[3]

Many today have either forgotten or never knew that at one time, both federalists and anti-federalists were very pro-freedom and liberty, as were both Republicans and Democrats. Many have also forgotten or never knew that Ronald Reagan was also a Democrat for most of his life, until as he put it, the Democratic Party left him. As time passed, the nation was being systematically driven further and further left in political ideology. The Democratic Party was first to be consumed by democratic socialists, but the Republican Party was also targeted for global influence and consumption.

Kent continued, "What any straight story of politics must show, of course, is that the power of political machines and political bosses is exactly equal to the tolerance of the people, that the extent of their domination and control is accurately measured by the indifference and ignorance of the voters, that it is the enormous number of non-voters who make powerful political organizations possible."[4]

It would be almost a hundred years later that the American voters would begin to relearn exactly what Kent had written about a long time ago. In part, this is due to the fact that Kent's books had been removed from public view and broad circulation decades ago. History repeats itself only when the people no longer know history.

Despite never having heard of Frank Kent or ever having read his works, the American people were being forced to relearn everything he attempted to record for all posterity all the way back in 1923. They were forced to return to the fundamentals of self-governance by process of elimination, even though they were not really aware of what they were doing, how to do it, or why.

The American people tried to take the path of least resistance, what they thought would be a quick, easy and painless solution to the demise of their country, once they saw just how fast the Obama administration was going to dismantle the constitutional republic.

First, *the people* tried to place the purse strings under the command and control of Republicans in 2010, thinking that they would simply defund the ongoing destruction of the country under the heavy-handed democratic socialism of the Obama regime. When House Republicans failed to defund any of Obama's destructive agenda, the people tried the next easiest thing: placing the power of the U.S. Senate under Republican control in 2014. Surely, they thought, with Republicans in control of both congressional chambers, this would solve the problem. That failed too.

As a result, the people were now convinced that no matter how much power Republicans were given in Washington, D.C., the train was going to remain on a collision course with history. The process of elimination had begun and *the people* were forced to look elsewhere, outside of either political party and certainly outside Washington, D.C. for any real solutions.

The people wanted the House to defund the destruction, but House Republicans would not. They wanted both the House and Senate to impeach Obama for numerous well-known and well-documented impeachable acts, including acts of tyranny and treason, but they would not. *The people* wanted their state governments to protect them from an overbearing federal government that had become destructive of freedom, liberty, national security, sovereignty, peace and tranquility, by enforcing the 10th Amendment (States Rights), but none would have the courage to do so. They wanted the judicial branch to rein in the executive branch that congressional Republicans had already failed to rein in, only to learn that the judicial branch was a mere political extension of the executive branch.

Next they would try to advance who they thought might be the most constitutionally grounded "conservative" in the 2016 GOP primaries, in search of a real pro-American candidate who they believed would fight *all of the D.C. establishment* on both sides of the political aisle, for the future of freedom and liberty. They were beginning to return to the basics, without really understanding why. But then, they witnessed the GOP establishment's unprecedented attempts to control the outcome of the GOP primaries in open overt opposition to the very visible will of *the people*, as demonstrated by a record primary turnout in state after state, all of it gathering steam behind what would soon become known as the *Trump revolution.*

> *This lack of appreciation of what the primaries actually mean, and the general neglect to participate in them, play directly into the hands of the machine. It makes it ridiculously easy for the machine, through the precinct executives, to control the situation. It actually permits the machine to run the country.* — Frank R. Kent[5]

Now, it must be stated that Kent's observations relating to the power of the precinct executive would have been true in 1923, when he wrote this passage. However, in 2016, much of the power had been stripped from the local, county, district, state and even national committee levels within the GOP. In top down establishment dictates to all precinct-level participants, these once-influential committeemen and committeewomen (as they were called until recent years) became nothing more than *yes men* (and women), commanded to do no more than the bidding of the party elites, following orders from on high and raising campaign funds for whomever the party elites dictated. The American voters were once again relearning this vital lesson of fundamental self-governance via democratic election processes.

> *To think that the general election is more important than the primary election, as most voters do, is to magnify the wrong side of the political picture. ... The fact that I wish to drive home now is that all over the country 99% of all candidates of all political offices are nominated as a result of a primary. The obvious and inescapable deduction is that in 99% of all elections, the choice of the voters in the general election is limited to the choice of the voters in the primary election. When the full significance of that statement sinks in, the tremendous importance of the primaries will be better appreciated.* — Frank R. Kent[6]

In 2016, American voters were figuring out by accident exactly what Kent told us in 1923: "It ought to be clear that the man who votes in the general election and not in the primary, loses at least 50% of the value and effectiveness of his vote as compared to the man who votes in both." [6]

This explains why American voters have been "holding their noses" in the general elections, choosing between "the lesser of two evils" for decades. That's what they were handed by the people who showed up to vote in the primaries.

Making matters even worse, the Republican Party had

increasingly adopted an "open primary" structure and although many registered GOP voters failed to participate in the GOP primaries, many Democrats and independents often voted in Republican primaries in order to eliminate any real Republicans from the general election ballot. Then, come November, they voted for the DNC candidate in the general election.

But in 2016, a record number of voters turned out in the primaries, and the vast majority would cast a ballot for someone who was a D.C. establishment "outsider."

> *It also ought to be plain that the man who poses as an independent in politics and declines to affiliate with either party, thus disqualifying himself as a primary voter, has greatly lessened his individual importance as a political factor as well as added to the strength of the machine.* — Frank R. Kent[7]

At the time Kent wrote this, open primaries were not yet in vogue. Today, the vast majority of American voters are registered as independents. While thinking they are fighting back against "the man" in this move, in truth, they were trained to do this by the establishment. The establishment wanted the most *conservative voters* to leave the party and take independent status, thereby disqualifying themselves from voting in closed GOP primaries, leaving those primary choices to more moderate primary voters. They also wanted Democrats to be able to vote in open GOP primaries as independents. By both measures, the establishment was able to hijack the Republican Party from Republican voters and move the party further and further left until it would become indistinguishable from the Democratic Party.

Years later, the results of these maneuvers left the independents increasingly (and falsely) convinced that they had made the right choice, in a self-fulfilling prophecy. Primary after primary resulted in predictably poor candidates to choose from in the general elections, due to moderate primary voters. Kent warned of this too: "WHY PRIMARIES ARE IMPORTANT — boiled down, it comes to this: so long as the primaries are controlled by the machine, the general election voter, no matter how independent he (or she) may be, 99% of the time is limited in his choice to two machine selections. There is no getting away from that fact."[8]

As the people lost faith in the Party machinery they had already left via their independent status, or general lack of engagement in the GOP primary process even as GOP voters, they would become increasingly convinced that only a new party machine or third-party initiative could ever solve the problem that now existed in both major parties.

The first problem with this idea is that no third party ever has been or ever will be viable in the United States. The reason is that when people leave one of the two major parties, they do not congregate in any competitive third alternative. Instead, they are politically in the wind, like dandelion seeds in a spring storm, scattered across a field of no less than 50 third party alternatives, none of them able to compete with the two major parties.

Once again, the establishment machine had found another useful tool to retain control of the electorate. They were able to use independent third party voters to divide the electorate to their own advantages. This was very visible in the 1992 and 1996 elections when the most successful third party candidate in U.S.

history, Ross Perot, helped the establishment seat Bill Clinton in the White House when Perot took 19% of the GOP vote in 1992 and 8% in 1996.

It seemed that no matter what the American electorate tried, nothing worked. In fact, the more creative or "outside the box" (aka outside the two parties) the voters became, the more elections they lost and their country along with it. The electorate had been triangulated. Every move they made, played right into the hands of the establishment elites.

However, by 2016, the electorate was forced to wise up and get engaged. All else having failed, they had no choice but to return to the basics and force their will upon the establishment by simply swamping the primary elections in record numbers. When they did that, the establishment lost control of the GOP as Trump became ever more powerful as a GOP candidate, gaining power every time the people saw the establishment work to derail him.

On the DNC side of the race, Sanders was challenging Hillary Clinton for the Democratic nomination and his supporters were becoming violent in their efforts to force the nation even further into Marxist policies. Sanders' supporters were largely young college-age kids who were never taught proper history under the government-controlled K-12 curriculum or on college campuses from professors who had been radical 1960s peaceniks. Had they been, they would know that the very policies Sanders represents have bankrupted nations and left millions hungry all over the world. They don't know that a simple hamburger costs $170 in Venezuela today, or that Brazil and much of Europe is bankrupt because they have spent more in social programs than any society can possibly produce.

Meanwhile, on the GOP side of the race, the people who knew that it was free-market capitalism that made America the greatest, most prosperous and powerful nation on earth were seeking an anti-politician candidate with a successful track record of American-style accomplishments. They were looking for the exact opposite of what Sanders, Clinton, Obama and the do-nothing GOP Congress had to offer. They were seeking real *hope and change,* American style. They intended to Trump the GOP and then the country.

Most of them had never heard of Frank Kent, nor had they ever read any of his writings. But by process of elimination, they found themselves right where Kent had predicted, doing exactly what he had written about almost a hundred years ago. *The people* would have to regain control of their party and the federal government. They would do it by taking action at the primary level, swamping the GOP establishment at the polling booth, making it impossible for the GOP elites to control the outcome of the 2016 elections, as they had successfully done for so many years before.

As in 1980, when the people chose another D.C. outsider, Ronald Reagan, to shake up the establishment, the people were out to shake up D.C. again. They knew they had to go outside of the D.C. establishment to find such a candidate and they knew they had to find someone who was successful outside of politics, not someone who became wealthy as a result of political office.

Seventeen GOP candidates tossed their hats into the ring. But only one would be supported by the vast majority of Americans who had had enough of D.C. politics as usual. The people made it personal and they took the fight away from D.C. to the local level, in a truly organic, grassroots bottom-up groundswell of active anger. This time, their efforts could not be ignored, shouted down, or overcome by inside-the-Beltway "experts" who for years had chosen the people's leaders.

Was Donald Trump going to be everything they had hoped? Only time would tell. But the people had lost all faith and hope in everyone else. Trump would become their last peaceful effort to retake control of their party and their country.

The counter-revolution set in motion decades ago and now in control of the people's government, would finally meet the opposition. The counter-revolution was about to be engaged by the Trump revolution and no matter how much people wanted it to be all about Trump, it was all about much more than Trump. It was about the very survival of a once-great nation. It had become a matter of life and death. Push had come to shove and the people were no longer willing to remain a *silent majority* on the sidelines.

If they lacked the power to reclaim control of their party, then there was no hope that they had the power to regain control of their country. The proverbial writing was on the wall: The nation was in distress. Only *the people* could save it and to do it peacefully, they would first have to retake control of one of the two major parties.

The anti-American counter-revolution had just met the *new American revolution*. A seismic political shift of cataclysmic proportions was underway. America was going to be constitutional, free, sovereign and secure again, or it was going down in a blaze of glory!

Old lessons of freedom and liberty, self-governance by way of a constitutional republic, were being learned again. It is true that necessity is the mother of invention. When all else fails, always study history and return to the fundamentals, the foundations of freedom, liberty and effective self-governance. Despite being a bit dusty from decades of neglect, the Constitution, Bill of Rights and Declaration of Independence still stand as the supreme law of this land. Their principles and values are as solid today as they were when they were written and ratified. There was no need to reinvent the wheel. Reinforcement of existing foundations and laws was the right solution and this is what Trump was promising.

Whether or not Trump will deliver on those promises is yet to be seen. But at least his promises are right and Trump is not part of the problem. Maybe he can be part of the solution. Desperate times call for desperate measures. Trump is a wild card, but a worthy gamble under the current circumstances. He is not without risk — but he is also offering America's best hope.

Counter-Revolution by Evolution
CHAPTER III

Contrary to daily media criticisms claiming that Trump is single-handedly upsetting everyone's apple cart by entering the 2016 presidential race and becoming the Republican Party front runner, he is not the foundation for the revolution growing across America behind his campaign. It is *the people* who are creating and fueling the Trump phenomenon. They are fed up with everyone in Washington, D.C., the never-ending federal overreaches of power, the Obama effort to "fundamentally transform America" into a member of the global secular socialist commune and the gutless Republicans in Congress who have done absolutely nothing in either chamber to disrupt the ongoing dismantling of the constitutional republic.

The American people are rising in the new revolution against a global counter-revolution that has been waging war against America from within for at least a hundred years, in every facet of American government, academia, media and even religion.

The most self-destructive era in American history started during the Wilsonian period, wherein the mechanisms and machinery designed to forever protect and preserve individual freedom and liberty became twisted into a national central power structure destructive of those ends.

Before there would be a rising organic revolution to defend the U.S. Constitution, the Bill of Rights and the American way of life, there was first a counter-revolution to destroy America. Some would call it a velvet counter-revolution, largely quiet, moving in small incremental deliberate stages, through the labor movement, academia, the mass media, Hollywood, politics, the legal system and even churches. The shift from individual rights to collectivism was on the move in all facets of American life.

Before the ink was dry on the U.S. Constitution, foreign interests had set their sights on destroying the new nation. For more than 200 years, no foreign country had the power to achieve that lofty goal by direct confrontations with the United States. Only U.S. leaders could achieve such goals and only from within. Through the Charters of Freedom established by the Founders, America had gone from birth to the most prosperous, generous and powerful nation ever known to mankind. In short, America had become the envy of the world, a beacon of hope for all who craved freedom and liberty, through the toil and sacrifices of the American people. But as a result, it had also become a threat to all who craved power over others.

After the Cold War and the fall of the Soviet Empire, America stood alone as the only economic and military superpower in the world, and the world was not going to allow it to remain that way. Russia, China, Britain, the European Union and the Middle East would soon seek to challenge the United States. But not until after they could weaken the United States from within.

World War II was the last war America would win. In fact, it was the last war declared by Congress, and the last war America would allow itself to win because its political leaders and a growing number of citizens were fast buying into the "anti-imperialist" views toward their own country. After the end of WWII, the nation had already begun a socio-political shift from a deep-seated American pride to that of a global peacemaker and apologist for American supremacy — which America's enemies falsely labeled "imperialism."

The "anti-imperialist" movement would soon after take shape inside America, organized and galvanized by the anti-war factions opposed to the Vietnam War. Instead of declaring, supporting and winning wars in defense of freedom and liberty, here and abroad, the nation would begin to tear itself apart in an internal conflict between two segments of the population: "the Greatest generation," still willing to spill blood for freedom and liberty — and Americans of newer generations, only willing to spill American blood in their effort to "fundamentally transform" the nation into something it was never intended to be.

America went from declaring and winning wars to engaging in undeclared police actions, interfering in civil wars in foreign sovereign nations, deposing foreign dictators and making unwarranted and unwise attempts at nation building. All of it was intended to appease a growing "anti-imperialism" segment of the U.S. population that spent its time assaulting soldiers sent by politicians to do a job for the nation and undermining fundamental American principles and values. Americans were being systematically turned against America, through private counter-revolution activist orga-nizations like the Weather Underground, working in concert with and often funded by U.S. federal agencies seeking increasing central power.

By the 1960s, the "make love not war" peacenik crowd on college campuses was being co-opted by an anti-American count-er-revolution, from both outside and within our own government. All counter-revolutions target young prospective supporters because the young are full of energy and utopian ideas, and not much else yet. The young are an easy target for indoctrination, including social engineering designed to transform society in order to transform a nation. They are wide-eyed and eager for someone to teach them. During the same time, parental rights were being stripped from parents as the nuclear family was under assault. Before long, Mom and Dad would proudly send their children off to college, often to see total strangers return.

Counter-revolutionaries with their sights set on destroying the constitutional republic knew that above all else, they had to target the young, win their hearts and minds, convincing them that America is an "evil imperialist empire" full of capitalist greed, racism, homophobia, sexism and violent intrusions into foreign lands. At the same time, they needed to convince these young people that the failed concepts of Marxism, socialism and totali-tarianism are the future for peace, equality and tranquility, a new "progressive" idea.

Unlike past efforts by numerous foreign agents to accomplish the same feat, this time, there would be a very well organized and concerted effort that had taken its time to lay out a strategy almost impossible for the people to defend against. This time, the American fifth column, sympathizers to foreign anti-American elements operating inside the country, would co-opt young Americans to their cause by appearing to champion the special interests of numerous minority groups.

A group of anti-American counter-revolutionaries led by an organization named the Weather Underground had drafted and circulated an organizational manifesto titled *Prairie Fire — The Politics of Revolutionary Anti-Imperialism and a Political Statement of the Weather Underground.* It was a communist manifesto written by devoted communists for devoted communists. In their words (not ours), "Here is *Prairie Fire,* our political ideology— a strategy for anti-imperialism and revolution inside the imperial U.S."[1]

The nation was about to evolve in ways most people had never imagined. Through incremental usurpations of power and academic revisions of history and the language, anti-American sentiments would spread like wildfire across college campuses, until the day would arrive when a majority of college students would openly support an avowed communist, Democrat Bernie Sanders, for President. It was akin to blind sheep supporting a known wolf.

Its creators wrote, "*Prairie Fire* is written to communist-minded people, independent organizers and anti-imperialists; those who carry the traditions and lessons of the struggles of the last decade, those who join in the struggles of today."

Community organizing sounded so innocuous at the time, but it now proves to be an extraordinarily treacherous activity. The kinder, gentler marketing of communism as a "progressive" movement was taking hold in the hearts and minds of the young, until American kids would quote *Mother Jones,* the longest-standing communist publication in America, as if it were an American history book.

Again, from *Prairie Fire:*

> *We are a guerrilla organization. We are communist women and men, underground in the United States for more than four years. We are deeply affected by the historic events of our time in the struggle against US imperialism. Our intention is to disrupt the empire — to incapacitate it, to put pressure on the cracks, to make it hard to carry out its bloody functioning against the people of the world, to join the world struggle, to attack from the inside. Our intention is to engage the enemy — to wear away at him, to harass him, to isolate him, to expose every weakness, to pounce, to reveal his vulnerability. Our intention is to encourage the people — to provoke leaps in confidence and consciousness, to stir the imagination, to popularize power, to agitate, to organize, to join in every way possible the people's day-to-day struggles. Our intention is to forge an underground, a clandestine political organization engaged in every form of struggle, protected from the eyes and weapons of the state, a base against repression, to accumulate lessons, experience and constant practice, a base from which to attack.*

The critical importance of that reference is this: The people who wrote this manifesto almost 50 years ago are the people in control of the United States federal government today. These people are the anti-American counter-revolutionaries and this manifesto was their strategy for destroying the United States from within.

These people started their counter-revolution against America 50 years ago. Today, they sit at the helm of every federal office and agency, every news outlet, many U.S. corporations and numerous international organizations like the United Nations and NATO. They are even in charge of the most powerful social media operations from Google to Twitter to Netroots Nation and well beyond.

Prairie Fire — The Politics of Revolutionary Anti-Imperialism (1974).

Many have heard of Saul Alinsky's *Rules for Radicals*[2] and the Cloward-Piven strategy[3] for bringing America to her knees by overloading the social welfare system until the nation would be bankrupt. Now they have watched as the strategy unfolds. Likewise, many self-proclaimed conservatives are familiar with — and even battling — *the UN's Agenda* 21[4] and *U.S. Global Governance by 2025*.[5] But very few of those well-meaning citizens know who and what is behind these initiatives, much less the fact that they are all just pieces to a much larger puzzle. Each one is part of a concerted strategy found in the manifesto known as *Prairie Fire*.

The basic idea is that people, nations and governments evolve over time. Everything on earth is in a constant state of change. Nothing stays the same for any length of time. The questions are what is changing, who is changing it and in what direction are things changing? Are we becoming a stronger constitutional republic, more free, more prosperous through our own productivity and growth as a people and a nation? Or are we being "fundamentally transformed" into something quite different?

Since the beginning of time, evil has always been at war with good. Tyranny has always been at war with freedom. While Americans slept calmly in their comfortable complacency, others were busy strategically planning for how they would strip Americans of their birthright to the greatest free nation on earth—without firing a single shot. To transform America, they only had to transform American society, alter the demographics and public sentiments of the American electorate and *the people* would eventually vote themselves into bondage.

As Joseph Stalin is reported to have said, *"America is like a healthy body and its resistance is threefold: its patriotism, its morality and its spiritual life. If we can undermine these three areas, America will collapse from within."*[6]

The Communist Manifesto from the 1950s was being followed with quiet precision:[7]

The Communist Manifesto, by Friedrich Engels and Karl Marx (1848).[8]

THE COMMUNIST MANIFESTO

1. U.S. acceptance of coexistence as the only alternative to atomic war.

2. U.S. willingness to capitulate in preference to engaging in atomic war.

3. Develop the illusion that total disarmament by the United States would be a demonstration of moral strength.

4. Permit free trade among all nations regardless of Communist affiliation and regardless of whether or not items could be used for war.

5. Extension of long-term loans to Russia and Soviet satellites.

6. Provide American aid to all nations regardless of Communist domination.

7. Grant recognition of Red China. Admission of Red China to the U.N.

8. Set up East and West Germany as separate states in spite of Khrushchev's promise in 1955 to settle the German question by free elections under supervision of the U.N.

9. Prolong the conferences to ban atomic tests because the United States has agreed to suspend tests as long as negotiations are in progress.

10. Allow all Soviet satellites individual representation in the U.N.

11. Promote the U.N. as the only hope for mankind. If its charter is rewritten, demand that it be set up as a one-world government with its own independent armed forces.

12. Resist any attempt to outlaw the Communist Party.

13. Do away with all loyalty oaths.

14. Continue giving Russia access to the U.S. Patent Office.

15. Capture one or both major political parties in the United States.

16. Use technical decisions of the courts to weaken basic American institutions by claiming their activities violate civil rights.

17. Get control of the schools. Use them as transmission belts for socialism and current Communist propaganda. Soften the curriculum. Get control of teachers' associations. Put the party line in textbooks.

18. Gain control of all student newspapers.

19. Use student riots to foment public protests against programs or organizations which are under Communist attack.

20. Infiltrate the press. Get control of book-review assignments, editorial writing, policy-making positions.

21. Gain control of key positions in radio, TV, and motion pictures.

22. Continue discrediting American culture by degrading all forms of artistic expression. An American Communist cell was told to "eliminate all good sculpture from parks and buildings, substitute shapeless, awkward and meaningless forms."

23. Control art critics and directors of art museums. "Our plan is to promote ugliness, repulsive, meaningless art."

24. Eliminate all laws governing obscenity by calling them "censorship" and a violation of free speech and free press.

25. Break down cultural standards of morality by promoting pornography and obscenity in books, magazines, motion pictures, radio, and TV.

26. Present homosexuality, degeneracy and promiscuity as "normal, natural, healthy."

27. Infiltrate the churches and replace revealed religion with "social" religion. Discredit the Bible and emphasize the need for intellectual maturity, which does not need a "religious crutch."

28. Eliminate prayer or any phase of religious expression in the schools on the ground that it violates the principle of "separation of church and state."

29. Discredit the American Constitution by calling it inadequate, old-fashioned, out of step with modern needs, a hindrance to cooperation between nations on a worldwide basis.

30. Discredit the American Founding Fathers. Present them as selfish aristocrats who had no concern for the "common man."

31. Belittle all forms of American culture and discourage the teaching of American history on the ground that it was only a minor part of the "big picture." Give more emphasis to Russian history since the Communists took over.

32. Support any socialist movement to give centralized control over any part of the culture, including education, social agencies, welfare programs, and mental health clinics.

33. Eliminate all laws or procedures which interfere with the operation of the Communist apparatus.

34. Eliminate the House Committee on Un-American Activities.

35. Discredit and eventually dismantle the FBI.

36. Infiltrate and gain control of more unions.

37. Infiltrate and gain control of big business.

38. Transfer some of the powers of arrest from the police to social agencies. Treat all behavioral problems as psychiatric disorders which no one but psychiatrists can understand or treat.

39. Dominate the psychiatric profession and use mental health laws as a means of gaining coercive control over those who oppose Communist goals.

40. Discredit the family as an institution. Encourage promiscuity and easy divorce.

41. Emphasize the need to raise children away from the negative influence of parents. Attribute prejudices, mental blocks and retardation to the suppressive influence of parents.

42. Create the impression that violence and insurrection are legitimate aspects of the American tradition; that students and special-interest groups should rise up and use united force to solve economic, political or social problems.

43. Overthrow all colonial governments before native populations are ready for self-government.

44. Internationalize the Panama Canal.

45. Repeal the Connally reservation so the United States
     cannot prevent the World Court from seizing jurisdiction
     over domestic problems. Give the World Court jurisdic-
     tion over nations and individuals alike.

As most Americans attended the piano recital, the baseball
game, Susie's ballet class and the family picnic, others across town
were focused on how to destroy the foundations that made all of
it possible. Later they would come to ask why their own government treats them as strangers in their own country — why they
were now labeled "domestic terrorists" and "extremists" for the
mere mention of the Founders, the Constitution or God forbid,
the Christian Bible.

They were completely unaware of the fact that the same people
who wrote that manifesto for destroying America 50 years earlier
in *Prairie Fire,* were now running their government and writing
new definitions to old words, like American, citizen, terrorist,
extremist, progressive, law, alien, gay, marriage, truth, conservative and independent. They had even changed the definition
of freedom to mean "free stuff" paid for by the hard work and
sacrifice of others.

Those same people had already turned the election system on
its head. People not even in our country legally now had more
rights than legal American citizens. Even worse, once Barack
Obama seized the White House via massive unconstitutional
fraud, he started importing anti-American elements from all
over the globe, most of them from Middle Eastern countries that
Obama himself had turned into war-torn areas.[9] He gave rise to

the Muslim Brotherhood by toppling sovereign governments and fueling the Muslim caliphate, later imported to the USA under the guise of "refugee resettlement."

Seven years into a destructive Obama term, most Americans still did not realize that they had a foreign usurper in their White House, a fact concealed by both major parties and all of the U.S. press. According to an article in Brcitbart, dated August 2012 and titled, *The Vetting — Exclusive — Obama's Literary Agent in 1991 Booklet:* a promotional booklet produced in 1991 by Barack Obama's then literary agency, Acton & Dystel, states "Born in Kenya and raised in Indonesia and Hawaii."[10]

Barack Obama

Barack Obama, the first African-American president of the Harvard Law Review, was born in Kenya and raised in Indonesia and Hawaii. The son of an American anthropologist and a Kenyan finance minister, he attended Columbia University and worked as a financial journalist and editor for Business International Corporation. He served as project coordinator in Harlem for the New York Public Interest Research Group, and was Executive Director of the Developing Communities Project in Chicago's South Side. His commitment to social and racial issues will be evident in his first book, *Journeys in Black and White.*

When running for U.S. Senate in 2004, his campaign proudly proclaimed that Obama was the first Kenyan to serve in the U.S. Congress. The individual was in the Oval Office in direct violation of Article II constitutional requirements for that office. But no one in either party or in the American press would ever dare to confront this reality.[10]

Part of a 1991 booklet by Acton & Dystel.[11]

Though the American people were largely blindsided by events unfolding right under their noses daily, they were becoming increasingly aware of the reality that their beloved country was in very severe peril, all from within. And they were becoming totally convinced that not only would no one in Washington ever do anything to stop it — they were all part of it.

Both major political parties were now under global influence. Despite campaign rhetoric indicating political differences between the two parties inside Washington, D.C., the vast majority of party elites were working together towards globalization and a *New World Order* designed to end American security, sovereignty and supremacy in the world. Members of both political parties were indeed part of it. Empowering themselves was their only focus, once elected.

Over the course of several election cycles, it had become obvious that the "will of the people" was no longer a factor in U.S. elections. Party nominees were being chosen in advance by party elites. The primary processes had all been compromised into a mere circus sideshow designed to create the false impression that *the people* were choosing the next leaders of their republic and the direction of their nation.

With each passing decade, American voters were becoming ever more frustrated by the reality that no matter who or which political party was entrusted with political power, the nation remained on a steady track for the proverbial cliff. In election after election, the people were forced to choose a candidate they had come to call "the lesser of two evils." In every election, they were denied a voice in the primary process, unable to advance a true candidate of the people in a system controlled entirely at the top. Until NOW!

The counter-revolution to seize control of all republican election machinery of, by and for the people was nearly complete. The people could vote, but only for whomever the party elites wanted. If the people tried to override the elites at the polls, the elites would simply change the rules to the game in midstream.

Decades of this practice had resulted in a total collapse of public trust in the election process.

Even as we write this today, both political parties are rewriting their own rules to overrun the will of the people in the election booth. Both parties are being challenged by outsiders. Neither party likes it, and neither intends to let the people's voice win the day.

The Democrat Party will have a known criminal, Hillary Clinton, as their nominee and everyone knew it long before the primaries ever started. Democrats supporting Bernie Sanders are watching their own party bury him via their "super delegate" scam, as we speak.

Meanwhile, the Republican Party was desperate to steal the nomination from Donald Trump, the organic front runner in the GOP primaries. They were stealing delegates committed to Trump in several states, as the race headed into Wisconsin and Colorado where the real theft was expected to happen and did. But this time, it would prove to be not enough to steal the nomination.

As a result of it all, the revolt by GOP voters was growing and the organic revolution behind Trump had begun. The American people, Republican, Democrat and Independent, are now convinced that unless they stand together, here, now, behind the only true D.C. outsider in the 2016 elections, their country will be gone forever.

The name is Trump. But the revolution is the people.

Republican Party on the Brink

CHAPTER IV

George Washington, the Father of our Country and first President of the newly created United States of America, was a Federalist and the first to refuse a $25,000 per year salary for occupying the presidency.[1,2] The year was 1789, 12 candidates were in the race, 150 delegates were up for grabs and Washington became the first U.S. President with 69, only 46% of those delegates.

In 2016, 227 years later, 17 candidates entered the primary race for the Republican nomination with the party dictating that a candidate must receive at least 1,237 delegates to secure the nomination on the first ballot. Otherwise, an "open" or contested convention would ensue, and party elites would choose a nominee for the voters whose voice they would ignore.

It would be the largest field of candidates ever in the history of the Republican Party, or any political party in America for that matter. Divisions once only visible between the two parties and the two very different visions for America between them, were now becoming glaringly visible even within each party.

As 17 Republicans took aim at each other in a bid for the Republican nomination, the Democratic Party was also showing signs of great internal divisions. The party's presumptive nominee, Hillary Clinton, was facing a growing challenge from card-carrying socialist Bernie Sanders of Vermont.

By midway through the primaries, the two Democratic Party candidates would be running almost neck and neck, with Hillary Clinton holding 55.4% of the declared delegates compared to Bernie Sanders with 44.6%. The Democratic Party had developed a "super-delegate" process for controlling the ultimate nomination regardless of popular vote or declared delegate counts. These "super-delegates" would give Clinton a 62.2% to 37.8% advantage over Sanders, overruling the much closer delegate race among declared delegates and Democrat voters.

But the Republican Party has no such fail-safe stop-gap "super-delegate" system in place for hijacking a nomination. As we write this chapter, the Republican race had already narrowed from the original 17 candidates to only three: businessman Donald Trump holding 743 delegates (53%), Sen. Ted Cruz 517 (37.8%) and Ohio Governor John Kasich 143 (10.2%), before the New York primaries where Trump was sure to perform well.

Rumors of a forced or strategically planned "contested convention" aimed at denying any of the three remaining candidates the GOP nomination were flooding the news headlines and social media pages. Although George Washington became President with only 46% of the delegates, the GOP powers were now scrambling for a way to deny their own organic front runner the nomination,

despite Trump holding 53% of the GOP delegates with more primaries to go.

For years now, the Republican Party has seemed to be perfect-
ing the art of losing presidential elections. Ideological divisions
between stalwart conservatives and progressive centrists in the
party first showed signs of fracturing in 1992, when political outsider Ross Perot ran as an Independent, challenging George H.W.
Bush for his re-election bid. In the end, Perot grabbed 19% of the
GOP vote in the general election, clearing the way for Bill Clinton,
who became President with only 43% of the popular vote.

In 1996, it happened again as the Republican Party ran Sen.
Robert Dole, who also lost to Bill Clinton. Clinton won 49.24% of
the popular vote to 40.71% for Dole. The fly in the ointment was,
once again, Ross Perot, who grabbed 8.4% of the GOP vote in yet
another third party bid, the difference between Clinton and Dole
vote numbers. Again in 2016, the GOP powerbrokers are pushing for a third party challenger. Unable to stop the Trump revolt
by any other means, a minority of Tea Party followers appeared
united with a handful of RNC establishment insiders, vowing
to even vote for Hillary Clinton or Bernie Sanders if need be, to
defeat their own party's presumptive nominee, under their "never
Trump" campaign.

Back in the 2000 election, the Republican Party was scraping
the bottom of the barrel in the conservative talent pool, to say
the least. Sen. John McCain was expected to be the 2000 GOP
nominee, almost a crowned king by the powers that be in the
GOP. But GOP voters had already come to despise McCain for
his less than conservative record in the U.S. Senate and they had
other ideas in mind.

George W. Bush, son of President George H. W. Bush was the incumbent Governor of Texas at the time and the conservative money brokers behind the GOP preferred him over McCain. Bush defeated McCain by a 2-to-1 margin in the GOP primaries, with 62% of the popular vote and 1,496 GOP delegates, 84.9% to McCain's 13.8% of the delegates.

Bush went on to lose the popular vote to Democrat Al Gore but win the Electoral College vote to become the 43rd President of the United States. Yet it was very clear that divisions in the country were broadening, and the Republican Party had likely hit rock bottom in its talent pool of up and coming conservative candidates.

After September 11, 2001, eight months into the new Bush Administration, his cabinet positions not yet filled due to Clinton Administration funny business upon leaving the White House, the single largest act of war on United States soil occurred, and for a brief time, it seemed that the nation might unite once again in American pride and self-preservation. Soon, though, even the events of that horrific day would be used to deepen political divisions that would tear apart any sense of unity in the American electorate, or even within the two major political parties.

The 2004 election cycle was largely a referendum on Bush's handling of the 2001 terror attacks. The nation was demonstrating its desire to prevent further attacks on U.S. soil, while supporting efforts to confront the sources of Islamic terrorism on its own turf in the Middle East. John Kerry was no match for Bush in 2004, especially with his fellow *Swiftboat veterans* working around the clock to expose him for his anti-American views and traitorous habits.

This unity would be short-lived too. The Democratic Party regained control of both chambers of Congress in 2006, making Bush a lame duck President for the final two years of his second term, during which time Democratic policies involving low-performing mortgages forced upon the banks by government regulations, bundled into traded stocks and backed by Fanny Mae and Freddie Mack, were used to create a banking crisis that resulted in a recession and a near collapse of the U.S. economy.

Meanwhile, the Republican Party was still heading for the cliffs. GOP voters had dodged a McCain nomination in 2000, but would soon have "independent maverick" John McCain thrust upon them in the 2008 election cycle by the "expert strategists" like Karl Rove at the helm.

Reaction from GOP voters was unmistakable. McCain was such a bad choice that he was easily defeated by the nobody from Kenya with a totally blank resume, Barack Hussein Obama. He won by more than 10 million votes. Yet this debacle would do nothing to shake the unwarranted over-confidence of Republican strategists.

In 2012, GOP "experts" would pick another stone-cold loser, former Massachusetts Governor and father of RomneyCare, Mitt Romney. Miscalculating the sentiments of GOP voters yet again, the "experts" in D.C. forced upon voters another "independent maverick," whom the Party base now realized was a left-leaning RINO (Republican in Name Only). The Tea Party, which was largely made up of evangelical Christians, would have nothing to do with the Mormon from Massachusetts. An estimated six million GOP (evangelical) voters stayed home on Election Day in protest against Romney and Ryan.

The worst (unconstitutional) President in U.S. history would win his second term strictly because the Republican Party refused to run anyone GOP voters could actually support without holding their noses. The GOP power brokers had become so consumed with trying to hand-pick a candidate of their liking that they forgot to consider the GOP base. Either that or they had intentionally set out to lose presidential elections and had finally perfected the art.

Meanwhile, public backlash to Obama's first-term destruction of our constitutional republic resulted in Republicans regaining control of the House of Representatives in 2010 and the U.S. Senate in 2014 — both times on promises that were soon broken. Although Republicans were now in full control of the nation's purse strings and even both congressional chambers after 2014, they continued to behave as if they were a lame-duck Congress, entirely failing in their constitutionally mandated oversight of a lame-duck President.

The GOP "experts" continued to tell Republican candidates that they needed to shift further and further to the left in their policy positions in order to win elections, despite the fact that with every shift they were losing elections and the base of their party. GOP voters were becoming convinced that no one in Washington, D.C. represented the will of the American people. Instead, Democrats and Republicans now worked in concert to achieve the same goal: the demise of our once-great nation. No longer was there a dime's worth of difference between an R and a D. Both parties were now working together towards the demise of the United States as a sovereign nation and the rise of global governance, regardless of campaign rhetoric to the contrary.

As voters left both political parties en masse, claiming Independent status in record numbers, GOP strategists continued on their path to self-destruction. The party was fast approaching the point of no return. So was the nation.

By the 2016 elections, GOP voters had had enough. They were determined to set a new course for their party and the nation. They knew they would have to look outside of Washington, D.C. to find someone who would represent *them,* rather than the global interests being championed by nearly everyone in the nation's capital, without regard for partisan affiliations.

The people set out to Trump the election and with it the party "experts" and strategists, the money brokers who had destroyed their party and the federal government which had become tyrannical in nature and destructive of all intent and purpose to our constitutional republic. *The people* no longer saw either party or anyone in D.C. as a solution to any problem. They now saw all of them as part of a single runaway problem that would require an outsider to resolve!

The people were going to force real change, or they were prepared to let the Republican Party end up on the ash heap of history, just as the Whig Party had. It was time for the GOP to return to its pro-American roots or die a sudden death.

A Nation on the Brink

CHAPTER V

*W*e must now face the harsh truth that the objectives
of communism are being steadily advanced because
many of us do not recognize the means used to
advance them. ... The individual is handicapped by coming face
to face with a Conspiracy so monstrous he cannot believe it exists.
The American mind simply has not come to a realization of the evil
which has been introduced into our midst. — J. Edgar Hoover, former FBI
director.[1]

2016 did not represent a time when only the two major political
parties were on the brink of extinction. It marked a time when the
U.S. Constitution, Bill of Rights and Declaration of Independence,
as well as freedom, liberty, the rule of law and the nation as a whole
also trembled on the brink. Seven years into Obama's "hope and
change" and the "fundamental transformation" of America, and
five years of no action from Republicans in Congress, the nation

was falling off the cliff and nearly every American knew it.

In every way possible, the nation was coming apart at the seams. Islamic terrorism was not only on the rise all over the globe, but also was making its way into every peaceful city across Europe and being imported to the United States by an administration that was at a minimum highly sympathetic to Islamic law, and at worst, the head of a global Islamic caliphate.

The country found itself in worsening racial divisions fueled by Obama and the Democrats' desperation to maintain political power at the expense of any hope for racial unity and equality in America. Women were being pitted against men, blacks against whites, poor against rich, illegal aliens against legal citizens and even federal dependents against the middle class (now defined by the left as "rich"). Homosexuals and transgendered individuals were pitted against heterosexuals and the traditional family unit. Christianity and Christians were under direct assault from every other religious and secular socialist belief system. Like all foundations of freedom, true Christianity stands in the way of the global agenda.

Obama's reverence for violent Islam was causing a backlash from Christians who felt like unwanted strangers in their own country, despite accounting for over 70% of the U.S. population. Constitutionalists were being openly labeled "potential domestic terrorists" and "tin foil hat conspiracy theorists" for simply attempting to place the U.S. Constitution and Bill of Rights back at the foundation of a country once made the greatest on earth by those very principles, values and supreme law of our land. Alinsky's Rules were in full play.

As the Obama administration arms, trains and funds Islamic

terrorism all over the world, giving aid and comfort to groups like Al Qaeda and ISIS and rise to the Muslim Brotherhood, they work to disarm peaceful, law-abiding Americans. As they import illegal aliens and potential Islamic sleeper cells and grant them federal welfare and Social Security funds, they deny coverage and benefits to legal Americans, even when they are in life-threatening circumstances.

The left claims many Americans are "anti-immigration" when in fact, most of them are merely anti-ILLEGAL immigration and anti-national bankruptcy. Under the overt use of the Cloward-Piven strategy, the entire system is being overloaded with nothing but takers from outside until the producers inside can no longer produce enough to keep the nation economically afloat, sinking America deeper and deeper in unsustainable debt.[2,3]

The Obama Administration has pitted Hispanic gangs and the "black lives matter" movement against all law enforcement, making enforcement of our laws ever more difficult, while at the same time hamstringing U.S. soldiers on the battlefield through suicidal Rules of Engagement (ROE). The result is the highest casualty numbers at the lowest point of war engagement and the highest incarceration rate for soldiers accused of doing their jobs in battle. We are also witnessing the highest soldier suicide rate in U.S. military history, averaging 22 per day and worsening.

Bernie Sanders is shockingly—and frighteningly—popular among young voters, and that is mostly due to the hopelessness that both the Democratic and Republican Parties have caused. Americans are more frightened of their future today than at any time in history, including the Great Depression and World War II era. Millions of Americans are aware of the reality that joblessness in this country is not at 5% as the government and their media would have you believe. It is closer to 30%.

An estimated 40% of American adults are on some form of anti-depressant. About the same number are receiving some form of government aid just to keep roofs over their heads and food on their family tables. The national infrastructure has eroded to the point of collapse, despite massive spending which has driven the nation to more than $20 trillion in debt, with more than $120 trillion more in unfunded liabilities. Our national security capabilities are at pre-World War II readiness at a time in history when our republic is under the greatest threat it has ever faced.

And the "experts" still can't figure out why millions of Americans are lining up behind a self-made billionaire anti-establishment outsider who knows how to meet a payroll and still balance the books?

Freedom and liberty-loving Americans are simply desperate for a Trump card to play, a chess move that turns the tables on everyone who has shared in the systematic demise of the greatest nation ever known to mankind. The total anti-establishment movement unfolding in the 2016 election cycle is not about any one person. It's all about ONE country — OUR country.

The 2016 election cycle is not about one race, one religion, one economic class, one political ideology or one party or the other. It's all about ONE THING: the preservation of America and the promise of freedom. This nation can no longer afford to be divided by armchair politicos, government experts, career politicians or their strategists in academia and the media. We can no longer afford to allow people who have pitted American against American for decades to continue doing so at the expense of every American of every race, creed and color.

If we are no longer one nation, under God, united in defense of freedom and liberty — if the U.S. Constitution and Bill of Rights are no longer the supreme law of this land—then there is nothing left which grants anyone in Washington any authority at all over the people. Every Oval Office occupant, every member of Congress and every federal judge, including members of the U.S. Supreme Court, holds office at the pleasure and consent of the people as stipulated in Articles I, II and III. If the Constitution is dead, then so is the government it created and everything that document authorizes the federal government to do.

All bets are off. We return to the Declaration of Independence, which unequivocally states two vital points:[4]

1. *When in the course of human events, it becomes necessary for one people to dissolve the political bands which have connected them with another, and to assume among the powers of the earth, the separate and equal station to which the laws of nature and of nature's God entitle them....*

2. *We hold these truths to be self-evident, that all men are created equal, that they are endowed by their Creator with certain inalienable rights, that among these are life, liberty and the pursuit of happiness. That to secure these rights, governments are instituted among men, deriving their just powers from the consent of the governed. That whenever any form of government becomes destructive of these ends, it is the right of the people to alter or to abolish it, and to institute new government, laying its foundation*

on such principles and organizing its powers in such form,
as to them shall seem most likely to affect their safety and
happiness.

That document also acknowledges the realities of human nature:

Prudence, indeed, will dictate that governments long estab-
lished should not be changed for light and transient causes;
and accordingly all experience hath shewn, that mankind
are more disposed to suffer, while evils are sufferable, than
to right themselves by abolishing the forms to which they
are accustomed. But when a long train of abuses and
usurpations, pursuing invariably the same object evinces
a design to reduce them under absolute despotism, it is
their right, it is their duty, to throw off such government,
and to provide new guards for their future security.

As our Founders recognized, mankind can accept unfair treat-
ment for a long time — until the associated pain and suffering
reach intolerable levels. In 2016, the American people reached the
breaking point. They would make one more attempt to cast off the
shackles of an overbearing runaway federal government operating
well beyond any constitutional authority. This time, though, unlike
their forefathers in 1776, they would use peaceful political means
to accomplish their goal, if the powers that be would allow. They
would focus all attention on the primary process, even though in
the past, primaries were often ignored by the majority of voters.

This time, the people would attempt to Trump Washington,
D.C. No longer would they try to fix Washington D.C. by relying

upon anyone currently there. They would roll the dice, gambling on a total political novice with no prior experience in office, but a track record of building instead of destroying and profit experience rather than poverty expertise. They would risk their all on someone who did not become wealthy via political office, but rather became astoundingly successful despite government intrusions and interventions.

To walk the Republican Party and the nation back from the brink of extinction, the party and the nation would have to be Trumped! The man is almost incidental to the movement. The movement is quite by intent and the future of the entire nation hangs in the balance.

The Outsider vs. the Establishment

CHAPTER VI

Among the initial 17 GOP presidential nominees for 2016, only three were "political establishment outsiders": business mogul Donald Trump, retired neurosurgeon Ben Carson and former Hewlett-Packard (HP) CEO Carly Fiorina, although Fiorina had been a close comrade of Republican and Democrat "insiders" for many years. The other 14 candidates were all Republican Party "insiders." Some were more popular with the political establishment than others, but all of these political beasts came from within the Republican Party ranks.

The establishment insiders were quickly eliminated from the race one by one, coalescing behind each other as each dropped out, all of them in open opposition to all political outsiders. Fiorina failed to catch fire largely due to her past failings at HP and her longtime association with Democrat candidate Hillary Clinton, dating all the way back to their college years together. Carson caught fire for a bit, but fell prey to numerous attacks related to his childhood mistakes and to underhanded campaign tricks from the Cruz campaign, which was stealing Carson voters from Iowa, until Carson was forced to drop out.

That left businessman Donald Trump the last outsider standing in the 2016 race for the Republican Party nomination, and that made him public enemy number one for the GOP and DNC establishment. The Republican insider field had also been narrowed from 14 to two: Sen. Ted Cruz from Canada and Gov. John Kasich from Ohio, both of whom should have dropped out long before if defeating the political left had really been their goal. While the two Democrat contenders were splitting their party's voters between criminal Marxist Clinton and Marxist Sanders, the GOP "expert strategists" were still busy trying to figure out how to deny the GOP nomination to anyone but their own hand-chosen candidate.

Throughout the primaries, Republican National Committee (RNC) Chairman Reince Priebus talked out of both sides of his mouth on a daily basis. He'd say, "one of the three in the race will be our nominee," (usually the people's choice of front runner with the most votes), at the same time, suggesting an eleventh hour "white knight savior" chosen by the Party elites without any voter involvement whatsoever at a contested convention. Priebus was eyeing a Republican Party insider to replace the people's choice in the GOP primaries as if he had absolutely no clue what kind of total collapse and backlash from voters he was playing with. The Trump revolt was intensifying by the hour.

Clearly, to the GOP establishment, the race was all about Party elites maintaining power over the Party and *the people*. They would battle the last remaining outsider who tried to upset the top-down stranglehold on power currently held by Priebus,

Ryan, McConnell, McCain, Graham, Rove, Bush, Romney, Kasich, Rubio and Cruz.

Now, everyone knows that Ohio Governor John Kasich had no chance of ever legitimately becoming the GOP nominee, having won only his home state of Ohio. Everywhere else he ran a distant third behind both Trump and Cruz. Can you even imagine some acceptable method of handing the nomination to a third place finisher who lost 49 of 50 states and denying the natural winner the nomination?

To some degree, Cruz supporters are correct in saying Kasich is playing "spoiler" for Cruz, and/or Trump, since there is no certainty at all who Kasich voters would turn to if he were not in the race. In numerous states, ballots have been cast for candidates who dropped out long ago. Many voters don't even pay enough attention to know who is or isn't in the race — nor do they pay enough attention to declared verses undeclared delegates. A vote for the latter is the equivalent of not voting at all.

Those who know the U.S. Constitution and Article II eligibility requirements for the Oval Office also know that Sen. Ted Cruz has a near zero likelihood of ever becoming the GOP nominee. If, by chance, he did, the Democratic Party would immediately destroy him in the general election over the very real fact that Sen. Rafael Edward (Ted) Cruz was, indeed, born a legal citizen of Canada and not the United States. They know, thanks to Ted's official documents, that Ted remained a legal citizen of Canada from birth until May 2014, when he officially renounced his Canadian citizenship.[1]

As of this writing, Sen. Cruz possesses absolutely no United States citizenship authentication of any legal type. As Ted has stated repeatedly, he has "never naturalized to the United States." Instead, Ted has claimed that he "needs no U.S. documentation of legal citizenship." This means the following facts have been documented and cannot be overcome in any eligibility claim:

Birth Certificate No. 332834 for Rafael Edward Cruz. Edmonton Dept of Health, Canada.

TED CRUZ ELIGIBILITY FACTS

1. Rafael Edward (Ted) Cruz was born a legal citizen of Canada.
2. Ted Cruz was, therefore, born under the legal jurisdiction of Canada, not the United States.

3. Canada did not allow dual citizenship at the time of Ted's birth in 1970.

4. Ted has never naturalized from Canada to the United States.

5. Ted remained a legal citizen of Canada from birth until May 14, 2014.

6. Ted possesses no authentic proof of legal U.S. citizenship of any kind.

7. Therefore, Ted cannot possibly be a legal citizen of the United States, much less a natural born Citizen eligible for the Oval Office.

8. Harvard Lawyer and U.S. Senator Ted Cruz knows it, even though his many fans do not know or do not care.

Even if Ted Cruz were able to produce any authentic U.S. documentation of legal citizenship, it would only prove naturalized citizenship, which would also disqualify him from the Oval Office. So, in the end, with both Cruz and Kasich in no-win positions, Trump, as the only *real* eligible outsider in the race, was the prime target for every candidate and everyone — Republican and Democrat alike — in the Washington, D.C. establishment.

Normally, the GOP nominee is pretty well known shortly after the South Carolina primary, the first primary in a conservative state in the RNC primary schedule. Not in 2016 however. From a purely mathematical standpoint, Kasich would have to win 1,094 more delegates in order to win the GOP nomination and only 879 delegates were still up for grabs as the campaigns approached New

York. Cruz would have to win 82% of the remaining delegates in order to become the nominee.

Certificate of Renunciation of Canadian Citizenship,
for Rafael Edward Cruz(May 14, 2014), Alberta, Canada.

But Trump only needed to win 56% of the remaining delegates available in order to win the magic 1,237 delegates. People wanting a D.C.-free candidate had no choice but to get behind Trump, who now had an approximate 90% chance of becoming the nominee, even before the New York contest.

Once again, this has nothing to do with endorsing Donald Trump. This has to do with much more than any one man. Every wildly successful person in America has a strong, healthy ego as part of his personality makeup. It's part of being a Type A personality, an achiever. The first step in being an achiever in life is believing you can do whatever you set out to do. Frequently that personality trait is erroneously interpreted as egomania or arrogance. In fact, it is usually nothing more than hard-earned self-confidence. This story is not a political endorsement of Trump the man. We do not believe that any one man will be the ultimate salvation of the constitutional republic. We believe that only a God-fearing people are capable of achieving that lofty goal.

Still, never in history has the Republican Party flooded its own primaries with so many candidates. But the bigger issue is the GOP power play supporting constitutionally ineligible candidates for the first time. In the 2016 primaries, Priebus and the Party powers not only allowed at least three unconstitutional frauds to run under their Party label, but they also supported all of them as if they were eligible for the office, without any regard for how GOP voters would react.

Gov. Bobby Jindal and Sen. Marco Rubio are both U.S. citizens by virtue of U.S. statute concerning the naturalization term "citizen at birth." Both owe their citizenship to their so-called "anchor baby status." Each was born in the USA to foreign parents. On the other hand, Sen. Ted Cruz, was born a citizen of Canada in 1970 and remained a legal citizen of Canada until 2014 when he officially renounced that citizenship.

The GOP field was also full of party has-beens like Bush and Kasich. It was full of wannabes like Santorum and Perry, both of whom had run and lost miserably before. But the shocker was the three blatantly ineligible candidates being supported by the GOP powers and their highly paid media machine. Jindal failed to get out of the starting gate and left the race early. Rubio hung around long enough to lose his home state of Florida in a landslide victory for Trump.

But how was a known Canadian citizen with no U.S. citizenship papers at all running second in the GOP race, despite knowledge of Article II ineligibility, tabloid stories of infidelity, main stream reports of mass cheating in numerous primaries and every other candidate openly calling the man a bald faced liar in every GOP debate? It was starting to feel like Obama 2.0: a freshman senator with zero accomplishments, who had never held a private sector job, with obvious ineligibility and a pattern of habitual lying, running second behind Trump.

There is no question that the Democratic Party would destroy Ted Cruz by simply disqualifying him early in the general election, leaving the path to the White House wide open for the Democratic nominee. So why is the GOP allowing a known fraud to even run on their label, much less to challenge the organic front runner for the GOP nomination? Is this how we *amend* the Constitution, now? Is foreign occupation of our Oval Office the intended goal?

Why were a number of once trusted "outsiders" all of a sudden working for the establishment "insiders" to derail the people's choice, Trump? Why were "Tea Party" people like Mark Levin, Glenn Beck and Erick Erickson of Red State, not to mention

Megyn Kelly and many others in the "main stream" news media, so blatantly anti-Trump and pro-RNC power? The national Tea Party leaders, many of whom tried to block Obama's entry to the White House in 2008 and 2012, were working for the Cruz campaign in 2016, as if the Constitution no longer matters to them, the great "Constitutionalists" that they claim to be.[2]

The line between "outsider" and "insider" was becoming increasingly difficult to identify. Public personalities whom conservative voters had relied upon for years, at Fox News and elsewhere, were suddenly carrying water for the "insiders," jumping from candidate to candidate as one after another dropped out — at all times making sure to oppose the only true outsider in the race, Donald Trump.

Fox News Channel's Megyn Kelly has almost single-handedly destroyed the conservative reputation of the cable news network, while Glenn Beck and Mark Levin — once conservative darlings made millionaires by the Tea Party since 2008 — were now openly saying they would support Democrat criminal Hillary Clinton for President, before casting a ballot for outsider Donald Trump. All the king's men and women were exposing themselves as nothing more than shills for the D.C. establishment.

As is usually the case, if you follow the money, you find out why people are doing things you thought you would never see them do. Nowhere is this truer than in American politics.

All the king's men and women were on task, well paid to promote the propaganda of the GOP establishment in their desperation to derail the people's choice, spending over $75 million in negative campaign ads aimed at destroying Trump. They were not personally engaged in trying to make the best choice for the country, nor were they engaged in any form of real journalism, finding and reporting truth, as the eyes and ears of the American people, mandated by their profession as alleged journalists. No, they were overtly peddling propaganda for the party powers in D.C. and they were being well paid for doing so.

In the end, many assumed to be political "outsiders" would be openly working for the establishment, not just against Trump, but against every American voter determined to "Make America Great Again." They were all working together, in concert, to make certain that America would never be great again. And they were doing it for mere profit and power motives.

All the King's Media

CHAPTER VII

The 2016 election cycle had become Machiavellian in nature. The term's namesake, Niccolò Machiavelli, was a 15th century Italian Renaissance historian, politician, diplomat, philosopher, humanist and writer. He is best known for the heartless, deceitful, unscrupulous and downright brutal form of political engagement made popular by his book *The Prince*.

Machiavelli embraced immoral behavior, dishonesty and even the killing of innocents as normal and effective in politics. He even seemed to endorse it in some situations.[1] *The Prince* gained broad notoriety when many readers accused the author of teaching evil, suggesting that Machiavelli was providing practical recommendations to all would-be tyrants, helping them to obtain and maintain political power by any means necessary.

Donald Trump, the outsider, is so despised and hated by all the king's men and minions in the media that at one point, Glenn Beck stated on open air he would love to stab Trump to death if he could get close enough to him to do so. One of John Kasich's campaign workers said Trump could only be stopped with a bullet to his head and Mark Levin was screaming from the top of his lungs in every Levin Show episode that he would support Hillary Clinton for President before he'd support the people's GOP front runner, Trump. In the end, these missteps would come at a high price.

Fox News was carrying water for the GOP establishment in the effort to force an "open" (contested, brokered, theft) convention in Cleveland, Ohio, by stealing delegates state by state, even after Trump won the delegates legitimately. Meanwhile, rumor had it that voter machine tampering was used to switch Trump votes to Cruz votes in Wisconsin in order to prevent outsider Trump from legitimately becoming the GOP nominee. In Colorado, *the people* would be allowed no say at all.

It is clear that GOP powers are very familiar with Machiavellian politics and the campaign strategies of tyrants and thieves. But they would not be able to carry out their plot to steal the party nomination without all of the king's media, who must work in concert with GOP leadership to conceal the backroom deals and underhanded tactics of a campaign to disenfranchise every American voter behind Trump.

It's no secret that the media outlets make huge earnings at campaign time, with viewer ratings climbing off the charts as the nation is glued to their TV sets to watch the latest news on how the campaigns are doing. Now that the nation is in perpetual campaign mode, the next beginning the moment the last campaign season ends, the networks and even secondary online media outlets have become addicted to the steady stream of revenue generated by the two parties and now the PACs and super-PACs.

Politics has become a 24/7 earnings bonanza.

But there is even more to it than that. Media stories are shaped to keep the revenue flowing—not to report facts to an audience dependent upon the media as their source of information they use to make critical decisions regarding the future of their country, freedom, liberty and the rule of constitutional law. *The people are now victims of a 24/7 propaganda machine not unlike that of pre-World War II Germany, which was responsible for the overwhelming election of Adolf Hitler, who then proceeded to murder millions of people who cast ballots for him as a result of the media machine that misled the German electorate.*[2]

A highly coordinated and well-funded "Dump Trump" (#nevertrump) campaign was underway. Reports of money changing hands with unsuspected establishment bedfellows were emerging on an hourly basis. As of this writing, we've had reports of huge sums going to individuals pushing the "Dump Trump" effort, from known establishment coffers to unlikely media personalities once trusted by many Tea Party voters.

The Daily Caller reported, "The Conservative Tree House blog exposed the financial nexus supporting prominent 'conservative' pundits to promote in their media outlets Ted Cruz as the last, best hope to block Trump in Wisconsin, a state considered by the Washington-based GOP establishment as perhaps the last establishment firewall to block Trump from the GOP presidential nomination."

On January 13, in an article published by the *Daily Beast* headlined "Pay to Play?" Ben Jacobs noted that *Politico,* in an article that now appears to have been scrubbed from its website, reported on how the GOP establishment sought to buy radio talk show host Mark Levin.[3] One of the buyers was none other than the Senate Conservatives Fund (SCF), a PAC founded by former Sen. Jim DeMint of South Carolina that backed Cruz in his 2012 Senate bid and in his grandstanding senate filibuster against Obamacare. SCF spent $427,000 to buy copies of Levin's four-year-old book *Liberty or Tyranny* to distribute to donors. No wonder he refuses to tell the truth about Ted Cruz and his constitutional ineligibility. Lying for Lyin' Ted is a profitable enterprise.[4]

Tea Party "Christian constitutionalist" David Barton of Wall Builders and Tea Party guru Glenn Beck are also involved in the money-making scheme through the pro-Cruz super-PAC Keep the Promise.[5] In the words of one report by Conservative Treehouse blog, "Establishment political operative David Barton not only runs Keep the Promise, one of the most prominent pro-Cruz Super-PACs, but he also serves as chairman of Glenn Beck's Mercury One charity. So, the next time you see Glenn Beck on his knees proclaiming that Ted Cruz is the 'anointed one,' deemed by God to be President of the United States, you might ask yourself if God also deemed Barton to put at Beck's disposal the millions in Super-PAC money he can funnel to Beck, as long as Beck continues to sing Ted Cruz's tune."

The reports go on to say that "even these political whores do not top 'conservative' Erick Erickson, founder of RedState.com, who funds his media venture *The Resurgent* with super-PAC money from the Ricketts family of Wisconsin, big backers of Gov. Scott Walker (who incidentally also endorsed Cruz)."[6] They are also funding the "Dump Trump" effort.

The amount of money being spent to disenfranchise conservative voters across America who have chosen a total outsider to clean up political corruption run wild in D.C. is astonishing. And we are not talking about the billions spent by well-known global leftists like George Soros or politicians from the Democratic socialist side of the aisle. So-called Republicans, Christians, conservatives and faux constitutionalists are behind this broad-based scheme to derail GOP voters and install a chosen messiah from the ranks of the D.C. insiders. It's a very profitable venture indeed for all the king's media minions.

As reported by numerous sources, but taken from a current *Daily Caller* piece, "ConservativeTreeHouse.com documented that the Ricketts family funded Our Principles PAC to the tune of $3 million in February alone. We should not be surprised when FEC filings show money from Our Principles PAC flowing to Resurgent Media, with the box 'Oppose Trump' checked off as the Erickson media group's purpose.[7] ... In addition to all of those in the Salem Media Communications network, along with Mark Levin, Glenn Beck, Ben Shapiro, Erick Erickson and anyone who is hosted on the various media enterprises they front for—all are paid shills dependent upon political graft."[7,8] And this would prove to be only the tip of the proverbial iceberg—a 'berg that would dwarf the one that sunk the *Titanic.*

TOP SEVEN PACS BEHIND THE "DUMP TRUMP" CAMPAIGN[9]

1. *Immigrant Voters Win* PAC — George Soros
2. *Our Principles* PAC — Marlene Ricketts, who is the wife of Joe Ricketts, founder of TD Ameritrade.
3. *The Club for Growth Action* — an arm of the conservative group, *Club for Growth* — businessman Richard Uihlein.

Founded in 1999 by Stephen Moore, Thomas L. Rhodes and Richard Gilder.

4. *Conservative Solution* — Marco Rubio's former super PAC. They've spent about $54 million so far this election cycle. Their top two donors are Citadel founder Kenneth Griffin and New York hedge fund manager Paul Singer.

5. *American Future Fund* — Nick Ryan — campaign worker for Rick Santorum

6. *Stand for Truth* PAC — supporting Senator Ted Cruz for president.

7. Hillary Clinton allies have organized a group of 22 liberal groups that plan to take Trump head on. The group will be headed by *Moveon.org*. Their plans include orchestrating large anti-Trump protests, possibly including protests held at the Republican convention, and other major cities.

To save the constitutional republic, one man and the people behind that movement will have to *trump* all the king's men and minions, who are spending billions to "Dump Trump." Once again, RNC experts are busy, disenfranchising millions of American voters and setting the Republican Party up for complete and total collapse. If the GOP powers succeed in the hijacking of the nomination, it will be the end of the Republican Party, as well as the end of the constitutional republic. A key question: How does Ted Cruz play into all of this?

Barack Hussein Obama stole the election and usurped the White House in 2008. He was a man from nowhere, with a totally blank resume, no history, propped up by nothing more than forged documents and an invented autobiography not even written by him, about a father he never knew and a dream that belongs only to the anti-American counter-revolutionaries who had birthed, raised and groomed Obama for the sole purpose of ushering in the demise of the United States of America.

Since Woodrow Wilson's day, the Democratic Party has essentially been the socialist party of the United States. Accelerating with the heyday of the Weather Underground in the 1960s, the anti-imperialist movement in the United States incrementally gained political power at all levels in all branches of government, until they would consume governmental systems from top to bottom, North to South and East to West. From sea to shining sea, the global leftists would be in control of everything by 2016.

It was no longer just a Democratic Party thing. The counter-revolution movement was now in control of both political parties, the labor unions, the mass media, the secondary media, social media, academia, the judiciary, federal, state and local offices, local network news rooms and even many evangelical churches, to include *new world order* Catholicism. There was nothing in America that had not been infiltrated with anti-American zealots working in concert to bring about the final demise of a great nation.[10]

Like Obama, Cruz was a man from nowhere, with a resume totally void of accomplishment, a man with proof of Canadian citizenship and no authentic proof of U.S. citizenship of any kind.[11] There was no apparent reason for the support he was gathering among the ill-informed electorate — except that these voters were no longer capable of being forever vigilant in defense of freedom and liberty, no longer aware of, much less ready to fight for the enforcement of the U.S. Constitution and Bill of Rights. Many were "constitutionalists" who knew and cared nothing about the foundations of freedom and liberty, but instead, were willing victims of the greatest political con job in U.S. history, the Cruz campaign.

The facts regarding Ted Cruz were very well known, but seemed to have zero impact on Cruz supporters. To whit:

UNDISPUTED FACTS ABOUT TED CRUZ

- Cruz was born a legal citizen of Canada on December 22, 1970.
- Cruz remained a legal citizen of Canada until May 14, 2014.
- Canada did not allow dual citizenship in 1970.
- Cruz possesses NO authentication of legal U.S. citizenship.

So, why was Canadian Cruz being allowed to run for the highest political office in our land, an office exclusively reserved for "natural born Citizens" of the United States? And how were so many unsuspecting American voters so easily hoodwinked into supporting a known fraud who was even more dangerous than Barack Hussein Obama?

America had arrived at a moment in history when truth was stranger than fiction, and the populous seemed incapable or unwilling to separate the two. The nation was working hard to place a second fraudulent usurper in the White House, this time one bearing the Republican label, and all the king's men and media minions were on board.

Everything was at stake. All of the marbles were in play and nothing was being left to chance. The D.C. elites intended to finish what they started over a hundred years ago with Wilson: the final destruction of the United States and the end of the American presidency. Once reserved for "natural born" Americans alone, it was now open to anyone, from anywhere, even those with NO U.S. citizenship authentication at all.

It was the eleventh hour, the closing scene in a 240-year-long play, wherein *the people* were poised to vote themselves back into bondage under foreign rule, once and for all. Could it all be Trumped?

Counter-Revolution
Meets Revolution

CHAPTER VIII

S ooner or later, any counter-revolution to destroy America was bound to meet a revolution to save America. 2016 seemed to mark that time in history when freedom and liberty-loving Americans were ready to make one final attempt to save their Constitution and their republic via the primary election booth, to alter the course of the nation and a government which had become tyrannical in nature, before abolishing it altogether would become the only remaining remedy.

The people's effort to "Trump" the D.C. globalist machine by using the GOP primary process to overthrow the will of the establishment with the will of the people would take the form of a political campaign behind political outsider Donald Trump. No one would be more blindsided by the goundswell of conservative electorate support than Trump himself.

Many conservative voters had appeared ready to draft Trump

in 2012, when Mitt Romney was the RNC's presumed *lesser evil* candidate for the presidential race. Trump was intrigued by the idea of running, but he ended those prospects when he announced in May 2011, "After considerable deliberation and reflection, I have decided not to pursue the office of the presidency. This decision does not come easily or without regret, especially when my potential candidacy continues to be validated by ranking at the top of the Republican contenders in polls across the country."

Since that date, many conservatives in America were in search of a leader to seize control of a GOP in steady decline. The once-clear ideological differences between the two national parties were vanishing, until there would be nearly no noteworthy difference between the two sides of the D.C. aisle.

The 2010 political landslide which returned the House of Representatives to Republican leadership under Ohio Representative and House Speaker John Boehner was quickly proving to be a fruitless victory. Grassroots conservatives had hoped to stop leftist destruction of the republic by simply closing the national purse strings in the House, defunding the Obama agenda and placing the Obama administration in what should have been a lame-duck status.

Instead, the Boehner-led House would simply continue to fund Obama's destruction of the republic, as if they were all working in concert toward the same end, despite making a public display of standing in opposition. When Republican seizing of the House failed to bear any fruit, conservatives focused once again on the 2012 presidential race, where the best option offered to conservative voters would be Mitt Romney, father of Mass-Health which later became the template for Obamacare, and his running mate and now House Speaker, Paul Ryan.[1]

Frustration and desperation increased in the conservative electorate across the country, and all hopes of conservative leadership were dashed by the prospects of a Romney-Ryan ticket. As a result, millions of conservative voters were left sitting at home in disgust on Election Day 2012, assuring the re-election of Barack Obama for a second unconstitutional term.

The failing Republican House leadership under Boehner, followed by the failed GOP Romney-Ryan campaign of 2012, left conservatives desperate to gain control of the Senate. They hoped that if Republicans controlled both congressional chambers, Obama would be placed in an absolute lame-duck status. Maybe Congress would even begin a process to investigate executive branch crimes of tyranny, treachery and treason.

However, the conservative electorate would be highly disappointed yet again, when the 2014 mid-term elections garnered Republican control of both chambers of Congress. Republican House members and Senators both continued to act as if they were in charge of a lame-duck Congress, instead of placing the Obama administration on lame-duck status by putting an end to Obama's continued destruction of the country.

By early 2015, growing distrust and utter disgust toward congressional Republicans was off the charts. Public approval ratings for the Republican-controlled congress dropped into single digits nationally. That was even below the 11% approval rating of congressional Democrats, also experiencing a total lack of public support from their own constituents. The disdain against all Washington insiders, a.k.a. "the establishment," was reaching a fever pitch across America, leading to the inside *Coup d'état* to unseat House Speaker John Boehner and resulting in his announcement to resign the Speakership and his House seat on September 25, 2015.

Unfortunately, although more conservative-leaning House Republicans had succeeded in removing Boehner from power, they were much less successful in replacing him with a fire-breathing take-no-prisoners conservative that both the country and the GOP were now in desperate need of. Instead, standard backroom deal-making placed Boehner-lite Paul Ryan from Wisconsin in the Speaker's chair. Soon, the people would be disappointed — yet again.

By now, it had become abundantly clear to nearly all conservative voters that all D.C. insiders were hell-bent upon retaining insider control despite public sentiments in the election booth and keeping the Obama locomotive of destruction on track regardless of which party controlled Congress. The mood of the people was quickly shifting from anti-Obama and anti-Democratic-socialist, to anti-establishment in its entirety. The people no longer trusted anyone in Washington to stand up for the rule of constitutional law, to stop the insane bankrupting of our nation, to derail the Obama agenda, or even slow it down by defunding it in Congress — much less confront the evil or hold anyone in the Obama administration accountable for anything.

The people had come to expect nothing more than grandstanding for the camera from congressional Republicans elected in 2010. Members of Congress like Louie Gohmert and Ted Cruz of Texas, Marco Rubio of Florida and numerous others, who had been placed into power by the Tea Party and once trusted by grassroots activists, kept themselves busy appearing in carefully crafted photo ops, online videos and empty-chamber filibusters that accomplished nothing. The people's faith in these individuals sank deeper and deeper into an abyss.

The Tea Party had given Republicans congressional power for six years and nothing had changed at all. The Obama regime was still abusing Executive Office powers, thwarting U.S. laws and protecting, aiding and abetting America's enemies here and abroad. Meanwhile, they were assaulting legal U.S. citizens and their constitutionally protected natural rights and continuing to drive the nation deeper and deeper into unsustainable debt that now threatens the very life of the nation's currency, economy and security — indeed, its very sovereignty.

House Republicans had campaigned on establishing a real debt ceiling to stop Obama from further bankrupting the nation. Almost without exception candidates had promised to repeal the unconstitutional Obamacare, along with numerous other crippling laws and illegal Executive actions. Some Republicans, like Allen West, even campaigned on freeing U.S. soldiers who had been imprisoned at Fort Leavenworth for simply following orders on the battlefield, but breaking suicidal Rules of Engagement (ROE) put in place by the Obama regime for the purpose of hamstringing troops on the front lines. But when the elections were over and the new Republicans were seated in Congress, none of those campaign promises were kept.

The people added the power of the U.S. Senate to Republican control in 2014 to ensure that both chambers together had all the power necessary to hold Obama accountable for refusing to faithfully execute U.S. laws and protect national sovereignty and security. The GOP majority now had control over everything from illegal immigration to Middle East refugee resettlement[2]— the importing of unvetted potential Middle Eastern terror cells — to the illegal release of Guantanamo Bay detainees[3]. What did they do about any of these pivotal issues? Nothing — except to stand down and watch as former Gitmo inmates returned to the battlefield to kill more American soldiers.

House Republicans opened investigation after investigation — into IRS targeting of Republican voters, businesses and organizations; the massacre in Benghazi; the downing of SEAL Team Six on Extortion 17; the Raven 23 incident in Iraq and race riots in U.S. cities fueled by the Obama administration's racially charged "community organizing" cabal.[3, 4, 5, 6, 7] They even launched an investigation into the gun-running to known terrorists across the Middle East, which gave rise to ISIS or ISIL and now threatened the safety and security of not only the Middle East, but most of Europe and the United States. Then they looked into direct administration complicity in massive bank fraud, all of it funded via our tax dollars by the Obama regime and rubber stamped by the Republican-controlled Congress. Oh, and did we mention the FBI investigation into Hillary Clinton's misuse of private servers to leak "CLASSIFIED" national security data?

One congressional investigation unveiled the fact that during our 16 years in Afghanistan, we have helped that country surpass the golden triangle in international opium exports. That "success" has fueled a re-emerging heroin problem in the United States on a level not seen since the 60s era of peace, love, drugs and rock-n-roll.

In short, NOTHING ever came from any of these congressional investigations! NOTHING!

The people had had enough!

In 2016, they were going to fight back one last time, peacefully, at the primary election booth. They would unify behind the only D.C. outsider with a stellar track record of executive experience and not so much as a hint of political experience on his resume. The people's choice for upsetting the establishment apple cart was New York business mogul Donald Trump.

Why Trump? Although his critics are many, most of them establishment insiders or wannabe insiders, the logic behind the Trump choice is more obvious than most might imagine. Namely:

WHY DONALD J. TRUMP?

- He is NOT a politician.
- He is NOT a "stinking lawyer."
- He is NOT from inside the D.C. Beltway.
- He is self-made and self-reliant — dependent upon and answerable to no one.
- He has a lifetime of executive leadership experience.
- He is fire-and-time-tested. What you see is what you get.
- He is constitutionally eligible to hold the office of President of the United States.
- He has proven himself to be a financial genius.
- He does not have a record of being politically partisan — and he does have a track record of being pro-American.
- He has a lot of skin in the game and he's putting it on the line to fund his own primary campaign.
- He is tough, brash and angry — just like the everyday Americans who are supporting him.

- He has brought companies through bankruptcy — and that would give him fire power to rescue the bankrupt nation he would inherit.
- He is the anti-everyone else in politics.

Donald Trump's supporters need no more reasons than those stated above to support the one candidate who they believe can and will upset the D.C. elite. For the Trump troops, nothing the critics can say in their political attacks against the boisterous candidate can change the fact that Washington, D.C. has become entirely destructive of the constitutional republic and only someone from outside the Beltway has any chance at all of changing that reality.

On the what-he's-not side of the ledger, Trump stood head and shoulders above all other candidates. But he also had attributes and experience the organic revolt would need to defeat the establishment politicians in Washington. Namely:

TRUMP'S PERSONAL ATTRIBUTES & EXPERIENCE

- He had built something of value.
- He was an unabashed capitalist.
- He had a reputation for being tough but fair in all his dealings.
- He had private-sector respect from his colleagues and competitors alike.
- He was known to be a man of his word.
- He was a financial wizard at a time when America needed a financial miracle.

- He was a proven leader in the arena of great executives.
- He was an unapologetically proud American.
- He believes in putting America first.
- He understands that in order for our nation to be powerful it must be prosperous.
- He demonstrates every day that hard work and good decisions pay off.
- He is known for surrounding himself with the best and brightest people.
- He hates politicians as much as his supporters do.

Are Donald Trump's supporters right? Well, they are right that no one from inside the Beltway today, on either side of the aisle, will alter the direction of our country in a pro-constitutional manner or direction. Whether or not a Trump presidency can accomplish all the stated goals of his supporters is yet to be seen. But he is making a good case that he can, and the people are willing to believe.

Make no mistake though: The Trump train is not as much about the man as it is about the truly desperate state of our union as a free republic. The fact that no one in D.C. has demonstrated any sign of pro-American leadership, even with Republicans in control of both congressional chambers, is ultimately responsible for the revolt in the GOP electorate that is fueling the Trump revolution.

The Trump movement is not an effort to destroy the Republican Party, as the "establishment insiders" claim, but rather to save it from the tailspin nose dive the party elites have been in ever since Ronald Reagan left office in 1989.

Like Trump, Reagan was an establishment outsider with executive experience, in his case in both private and public sectors. He also had a highly unapologetic pro-American message that was very much akin to "Make America Great Again."

Like Trump, Reagan was feared and attacked by all D.C. insiders on both sides of the political aisle, often wrongly labeled with epithets like warmonger, dangerous and loose cannon. When lambasting his critics, or calling out America's foes in the world, or even her "friends" in Congress, he was called "un-presidential." Reagan's campaign opponents also said he was "inexperienced" and "knows nothing about foreign policy or national security." Granted, as a Hollywood actor, Reagan had a more polished public persona than Trump — until he got fed up with mindless critics lobbing unwarranted and indiscreet bombs in his direction.

Reagan was feared, wrongly attacked and hated by as many people as those who loved and revered him. The idea that anyone can take a firm stand for or against anything without losing friends is a fantasy of monumental proportions. Real life just doesn't work like that. Ronald Reagan, who was a registered Democrat most of his life, and married twice, has been written into history as the most conservative president of our time. But he was by no means a hardcore conservative. As an example, Reagan was the first and last president to approve "amnesty" for over a million illegal aliens.[8]

On the heels of a horrifically failed Jimmy Carter administration, Reagan was just the breath of fresh air and firm pro-American leadership the country was seeking. In the end, Reagan proved to be a much better Chief Executive than even many who voted for him would have predicted. I remember House Speaker Tip O'Neill going after Reagan in a manner very similar to how Hillary Clinton, Nancy Pelosi, Mark Levin and Glenn Beck have gone after Trump today. But in the end, even Tip O'Neill became a fan of Ronald Reagan.

In 2016, Donald Trump is the people's choice to lead the United States out of the fatal condition in which Barack Hussein Obama and congressional Republicans have placed the nation. And like Reagan, Trump is taking fire from establishment insiders on both sides of the aisle, who much prefer the politically profitable but nationally fatal status quo.

The counter-revolution of the 60s radicals, intended to fundamentally transform America into a third world commune, has been met by an organic revolution that has risen in the name of Donald Trump. But because the RNC and DNC now work together to maintain the status quo in Washington, the Trump revolution will have to fight both sides of the political aisle to win.

Let the games begin!

Cloward-Piven, Alinsky & Democratic Socialism

CHAPTER IX

In the good old days, Americans fought communism and totalitarianism in its many forms abroad, from WWI through Vietnam, and even Islamic totalitarianism in the form of jihad in support of the global caliphate. But beginning with the Wilson Administration in the early 1900s, through FDR's "New Deal" and the emergence of "democratic socialism" *(the convergence of the Communist and Socialist Party USA movements)* based upon the eco-political theories of men like Karl Marx, Leon Trotsky and Vladimir Lenin, Americans would come to fight these same evil ideologies on their own soil, in their own society, from the halls of their own government, in the labor movement, on college campuses, in church pews and beyond.

The strategies of the anti-American superiority crowd who called themselves "anti-imperialists" from the 1960s through today, would carefully craft and execute a long-term strategy for bringing

America to its knees and melding the United States into a third world member of the global commune for the "greater common good," of course.

It is critical for Americans to grasp the differences among these factors:

ANTI-AMERICAN PLAN FOR DESTRUCTION

1. The driving agenda
2. The multi-faceted strategy
3. The tactics for advancing the overall strategy and achieving the stated agenda

---

The driving agenda is to bring America to its knees, to end American superiority and supremacy in the world and meld America into a global commune wherein all American wealth, property and assets can be used to benefit the world, with or without the consent of the American people. The same people behind this agenda have even spoken openly about the need for "mass depopulation" in order to gain "sustainable control" over private sector wealth and assets for "the greater common good." Some, like Microsoft's Bill Gates and famed anti-imperialist domestic terrorist William Ayers have openly stated that as many as one-third of Americans would most likely have to be killed in order to achieve their global agenda of "sustainable development."

Many today know this agenda by the title *UN Agenda 21*. But contrary to rampant propaganda, *UN Agenda 21* is not controlling the USA. The U.S. Federal Government controls the U.N. and before there was *UN Agenda 21,* there was *Global Governance 2025,* drafted by the U.S. Federal Government during the Clinton Administration. It later became known as *UN Agenda 21* for *Global Sustainable Development.*[1]

Agenda 21 is just one segment of a multi-faceted strategy for taking America to her knees. Before that came the Cloward-Piven Strategy of Orchestrated Crisis. This brainchild of two radical socialist Columbia University professors named Richard Andrew Cloward and Frances Fox Piven made its public debut in the May 2, 1966 issue of *The Nation* magazine. This piece of a grander scheme was designed to bankrupt our country by simply overloading the social welfare programs to a point at which private sector productivity and wealth would be unable to keep pace with the growing demand for social services, thereby driving the nation deeper and deeper into unsustainable debt until the country would go belly up.

It isn't national infrastructure or war spending that has driven the nation to more than $20 trillion in federal debt. It is massive increases in public dependency upon social spending, which is now more than 60% of the total federal budget, that is bankrupting the nation, just as it has many a nation all over the globe. This is not an accident or the result of ineptitude on the part of democratic socialists, who now make up the Democratic Party and the Obama administration, with the complicity of Republicans in Congress. It is by design, with very specific purpose and intent.

Saul Alinsky's *Rules for Radicals* is a tactical tool, a carefully crafted set of guidelines for leftists aiming to destroy the United States from within by creating and fueling social divisions and civil unrest. It was designed as the means by which "political correctness" would be forced upon the people to forever silence *the silent majority*, who would become subservient to all minority groups gathered under the global commune agenda.[2]

Saul Alinsky and his 13 *"Rules For Radicals"* (1971).[3, 4]

ALINSKY'S 13 RULES FOR RADICALS

1. Power is not only what you have but what the enemy thinks you have.
2. Never go outside the experience of your people.
3. Whenever possible, go outside of the experience of the enemy.
4. Make the enemy live up to their own book of rules.
5. Ridicule is man's most potent weapon.
6. A good tactic is one that your people enjoy.
7. A tactic that drags on too long becomes a drag.
8. Keep the pressure on with different tactics and actions, and utilize all events of the period for your purpose.
9. The threat is usually more terrifying than the thing itself.
10. The major premise for tactics is the development of operations that will maintain a constant pressure upon the opposition.

11. If you push a negative hard and deep enough, it will break through into its counter side.
12. The price of a successful attack is a constructive alternative.
13. Pick the target, freeze it, personalize it and polarize it.

The 13 Alinsky Rules are mere tactical tools for neutralizing the enemy — namely you, the freedom and liberty-loving American. While Cloward-Piven is a strategic plot to bankrupt America under ever-increasing demands for social services at the expense of freedom itself, Alinsky's Rules are carefully crafted tactics for keeping *the silent majority* silent while the global left worms its way into power at every political level. The two, working in concert along with other pieces of a grander global scheme, create a formidable force to be reckoned with, a powerful enemy inside the gates.

Both the Cloward-Piven Strategy and Alinsky's Rules were carefully chosen strategic tools for dismantling and "fundamentally transforming" America from within. The 60s anti-imperialists knew exactly how to manipulate American society and gain control of the population for political power. While the Communist Party USA and Socialist Party USA failed to ever gain political power under their overtly anti-American political symbols, they were able to gain control of the federal government via *democratic socialism* — a Karl Marx theory in which democratic systems could be used to move the nation into communism incrementally, as the people were systematically taught how to vote themselves gifts from the public trough, as if voting for free stuff would result in more freedom.

The democratic socialist theory is sold as "democracy in action," the "little people" claiming their "fair share" of the earned wealth of others by democratic process. The idea is to make the federal government a modern-day Robin Hood, who takes from the rich and gives to the poor. It is the marketing of the "entitlement mentality" that now consumes K–12 and college classrooms under Common Core curriculum standards, which teach new generations the alleged benefits of global communism and the flaws in American freedom, liberty and exceptionalism.

But as British Prime Minister Margaret Thatcher once said, "The trouble with socialism is that eventually you run out of other people's money." [4] She was right about that. Even worse, the very people promised a better future under socialism, the middle class, would be the group most damaged by the concept.

First, a free, productive, prosperous and wealthy country is a powerful country. A corrupt, entitled, non-productive and poor country is weak. However, the real fly in the ointment of the counter-revolution Marxist assault on America is the reality that you can only take from the wealthy that which the wealthy are willing to give. People are not millionaires or billionaires by accident. They become wealthy by the decisions they make, and those decisions include countless methods of protecting the wealth they have toiled and sacrificed to earn.

Obviously, you cannot take from those who have nothing to take: the poor, the needy, the truly destitute who may in fact deserve a helping hand or a leg up in life. In the end, there is no one to steal wealth from except the middle class. They have assets of value but either do not know how to protect those assets from government seizure, or are not wealthy enough to take the necessary measures to do so.

Marxism, or *democratic socialism,* also referred to as "progressive" or "liberal" political policies today, is sold as beneficial to the middle class, when in reality, it targets the middle class for government seizure and redistribution of their wealth. The rich will always protect their assets by moving them beyond the reach of the government, off-shore if need be, investing in foreign lands that are moving away from socialism in favor of *free market economics.* The poor cannot contribute to governmental wealth redistribution. That leaves the *middle class* to target for asset seizure — using those assets to purchase the political loyalty of those attempting to vote themselves gifts from the treasury, as low-income voters grow in number. As a result, the life blood of any prosperous economy is strangled by government taxation and regulation in the name of central confiscation and redistribution.

In short, the wealthy take their assets and move to a new playing field, leaving behind the middle class to pay for the underclass. And that is why Prime Minister Thatcher was right. Socialism will only exist until you run out of other people's money. Once there is no one left to steal from, the result of socialism is the collapse of an entire economy and the inevitable fall of a nation.

How did the democratic socialists convince so many Americans to kill the goose that laid the golden egg of freedom and prosperity? It was much easier than you might think.

All they had to do was employ what the anti-imperialist left set as their strategy in the late 60s and early 70s, under the manifesto entitled *Prairie Fire:* They had to pander to the individual special interests of numerous single-issue voting blocs, convincing these groups that the left would fight for their interests. That would cause each group to unwittingly join forces with the anti-imperialists and fight for socialism, as if Marx was the enlightened prophet of a treasure much more valuable than individual freedom, many having no clue what they were actually fighting for in the name of their single special-interest issue.

Women were brought aboard in the fight for "women's rights," (aka abortion on demand), Gays, lesbians and transgendered individuals were brought aboard in the name of "sexual diversity." Ethnic minorities were brought aboard in the name of "ethnic equality," as if America was not already the most ethnically diverse nation on earth. The poor were told they shouldn't have to work, sacrifice or earn a living. They were entitled to their "fair share" regardless of their unequal contribution to society.

Through all of this, American was pitted against American, until by 2008, voters would elect a President of the United States strictly on the basis of his skin color. This was an individual who presented no information about his true birth condition, background or job history — much less any accomplishments that qualified him to lead the most powerful nation on earth. Voters made history by electing the "first black president," who as proven by his own family history, was not even black.

Society had been dumbed down to the level where they would vote for a person strictly on the basis of his *race,* while at the same time, decrying racial factors in any public or private decision-making. The people would vote for someone they knew nothing about, just because they had been Pavlov-trained to "make history" rather than protect and preserve their foundations of freedom and liberty. Free stuff was becoming more attractive than freedom until a growing number of public dependents began to feel a diminishing sense of freedom.

The results were devastating to all of American society, as the nation watched their country driven to more than $20 trillion in unsustainable debt. The people were being intentionally divided and pitted against one another for benefit of the ruling-class elites. It is this counter-revolution against all things American that would cause the backlash from millions of Americans, revolting in a somewhat hostile takeover of the GOP primaries. Soon they would take on the federal government, which had long ago become destructive of the people and their *inalienable* right to freedom, liberty, sovereignty and security.

The backlash that became the Trump Revolution in 2016 was nothing more or less than a mass public reaction to far too many years of anti-American assaults on every American. The Trump Revolution would become the turning point for America, and it would engage Americans from all political stripes in one common goal: to make America great again.

Trump caught on early and devised what seemed a naive slogan, "Make America great again!" He chose wisely. Those four simple words expressed the will of millions of Americans who had become fed up with America being forced to be anything less than great! By 2016, Americans had become sick and tired of politically created divisions that labeled every American as either a willing fool of the left or a potential domestic terrorist tool of the right. An exploding number of voters just wanted to be American again. Donald Trump promised to make that possible, and even popular.

Leon Trotsky (1879–1940), a leading player in the
Russian Revolution of 1917 and USSR Commissar for the
Russian Army and Navy Affairs from 1918 to 1925.[1]

No More Democrat Party, No More Racism

CHAPTER X

Славянофильство, мессианизм отсталости, строило свою философию на том, что русский народ и его церковь насквозь демократичны, а официальная Россия — это немецкая бюрократия, насажденная Петром. Маркс заметил по этому поводу: "Ведь точно так же и тевтонские ослы сваливают деспотизм Фридриха II и т. д. на французов, как будто отсталые рабы не нуждаются всегда в цивилизованных рабах, чтобы пройти нужную выучку". Это краткое замечание исчерпывает до дна не только старую философию славянофилов, но и новейшие откровения "расистов". — Leon Trotsky[2,3]

The term "racist" arguably ranks as the most powerful word weapon in the Democratic Party's arsenal. But it was not made up by Democratic politicians. Nor was it invented by the liberal sociologists and 1960s-era Marxist college professors who hurl it around in reference to those they deem to be "anti-social" toward ethnic minorities and illegal immigrants. In fact the words "racist" and "racism" were coined by Leon Trotsky, one of the principal architects of the Soviet nightmare and the founder and first leader of the Russian Red Army.

When Trotsky used the term, he was referring to the Slavophiles, a group of traditionalist Slavic Russians who greatly valued their native culture and way of life, and wanted to protect it. Trotsky on the other hand, saw the Slavophiles and others like them as an impediment to his *internationalist communist* plans for the world. Trotsky didn't care at all about the Slavic Russians whom he claimed to serve. To Trotsky, these people who committed the "crime" of loving their own people and trying to protect their traditional ways were simply "backward" and others like them were simply "racists."

The anti-American left, which had seized control of the United States government from the national level to the state and local level over the past hundred years, had built all of its political power on the abusive manipulation of every minority group in this country and around the globe by using Trotsky's word invention (racist or racism) like a sledge hammer to create a "silent" majority in America. In other words, no one was simply pro-American or anti-Communism. All were just "racists."

For many years, single-interest minority groups fighting for rights based on such factors as race, religion, gender, sexual orientation and economic status were manipulated into supporting the eventual demise of the constitutional republic in favor of their narrow special interests, ranging from illegal immigration and "women's rights" to free cell phones. Americans were systematically pitted against Americans, not for the purpose of empowering these groups or individuals, but rather to empower the *democratic socialists* pretending to care about them.

But between 2008 and 2016 all of these special-interest groups were feeling the pain caused by the very people who claimed to fight for their causes—and many would begin to see the light. A political awakening occurred within these minority groups that had been tricked by power-seeking politicians into attacking their fellow Americans. People in these groups were beginning to shift away from their individual special interests, realizing that their personal well-being could never exceed the well-being of our country as a whole. And that country was clearly being torn apart.

America is and always has been a nation of immigrants, but its strength has depended on the fact that the culturally and ethnically diverse people who came here have blended into an all-American melting pot. Tragically, during the last half century or so, the political elite has deliberately strived to create cultural and ethnic tensions among races and socio-economic classes, preventing assimilation, that in the end only enriched its own coffers while destroying the classic American dream.

History has been rewritten to suit the political ruling class. It was Republican President Abraham Lincoln who freed the slaves with his Emancipation Proclamation.[3] It was congressional Republicans who voted for the Civil Rights Acts of the 1950s and 60s. But Common Core revisions of history have manipulated the black community into believing that Democrats, who fought openly against these things, were responsible for seeking "equality" for ethnic minorities in America.[4]

Since the mid-20th century, the black community as well as other minority groups were reliable voting blocs for the Democratic Party. But by the early 21st century, a growing number of minority bloc voters began awakening to the reality that *democratic socialists* were creating social programs designed to keep them on the plantation and far removed from the American dream.

By the 2016 election cycle, many of these once-reliable Democrat voters had shifted to Independent or even Republican status and were beginning to cast off the chains of bondage that always come as conditions attached to every government freebee. People who had voted liberal for years were now feeling the pinch of a nation in decline, a massive exploding debt, declining job opportunities, stagnant wages and an eventual end to all government social programs as the nation was being rushed toward economic collapse. The federal government was running out of other people's money, and the people left empty handed were those once co-opted into supporting *democratic socialism*.

In short, it was becoming obvious to all Americans that creeping *progressive socialism* was fast running out of other people's money, just as Margaret Thatcher had warned decades ago. America was no longer the great shining city on the hill, the land of the free, the home of the brave or the land of milk and honey. It was being systematically reduced to global third-world status in an economic tailspin that was the result not of mere incompetence, but of intentional strategic planning.

American conservatives who once believed voting Republican was enough to protect and preserve the golden goose, as well as people who once bought into the Marxist Robin Hood theory of "from each according to his ability; to each according to his need," were all turning on the ruling class that had placed every American in the crosshairs of total destruction. If these elites had their way, no American would live in freedom or liberty, and poverty would become universal (except, of course, for those kingpins calling the shots).

Since the 60s, the anti-imperialist counter-revolution had been destroying America from within through the institutions of local, state and federal government; the halls of Ivy League colleges and eventually K-12 public schools. Even Christian churches were infiltrated by people with a global communist agenda, teaching that Jesus was a commie who fed those in need, overlooking the other side of Jesus who overturned the money-changers' tables in the temple. The global evangelical movement was hijacked by the globalization movement, teaching Americans from the pulpit to accept every evil on earth, from sexual perversions sold as mere individual choice to illegal invasions of our country that would forever alter the voting demographics against the will of all American citizens.

It was not for nothing. To destroy the United States from within, they would have to destroy all American foundations. They would have to demolish the traditional family, create racial divisions, eliminate respect for life itself, import foreign interests, export American jobs and overload the economy with an ever-increasing number of takers and fewer and fewer givers. They would have to replace private charity with government-seized private assets and government handouts that only empowered the politically powerful. They would have to pit religion against religion, educated against less educated, poor against rich, race against race — until the social fabric of our nation was fundamentally transformed into an anti-American electorate ready to doom itself to suicide — to vote itself into bondage.

By 2016, pains associated with these anti-American endeavors was being felt by nearly every American. One by one, group by group, the people started to turn on the tyrants and the treacherous ruling class that had set the nation against itself. The people were now looking to overthrow the ruling class, without regard for partisanship, in search of a new way forward that would not only *make American great again* — it would also return to the people the freedom to determine their own destiny — without interference from an over-reaching and overbearing federal government.

The people were tired of racial, socio-economic and cultural warfare that benefited the ruling class, at great expense to every American from every walk of life and corner of the country. Of course black lives matter — so do white lives, oriental lives, Hispanic lives and all forms of human life, including the unborn.[5, 6] A rising tide raises all ships — and a receding tide grounds all ships. There is but one America, one American, one American English language and one American dream: freedom and liberty. All other ambitions and dreams for a fundamentally transformed America are anti-American at their foundations.

The people were ready to TRUMP the system. If possible, they would do it peacefully, gaining control of the Republican Party and the federal government through the GOP primary process. The Party powers flooded the GOP field with a record 17 candidates, many of them unqualified for the job, others not even constitutionally eligible for the office, most of them elitist Washington insiders. The party pundits did all they could to control the outcome of the GOP primaries. They pulled out every stop, spent every penny they could muster and pulled every dirty trick ever known to political warfare. Still, in the end, the D.C. elites were TRUMPED by the people. They were not able to stop the voter revolt, no matter how strong or underhanded their efforts. The people were going to make real changes this time and America was going to come first.

The 2016 election would not be about race, religion, gender, economic status or right and left in the old political paradigm. It would be all about right and wrong: America vs. the anti-American counter-revolution that had been destroying our country from within for more than a hundred years, no matter which political party held power.

It was time to look outside of the political class in both parties for solutions. It was time for an anti-establishment wild-card candidate who had skin in the game, a track record of successful executive leadership in the private sector and — perhaps most of all — a general disdain for the corruption and destruction by the political class, equal to that of the voters who created the revolt.

It was time to set aside all petty special-interest differences, cast off the chains of political ambitions and reclaim American-citizen control of the country while there was still a country that could be saved. It was time to TRUMP the nation — and the people behind the revolt were in no mood to take prisoners.

Things were going to change and anyone who didn't like it didn't matter anymore. In the end, Americans of every race, creed, color and political persuasion would join forces in the 2016 GOP primaries to reclaim their constitutional republic and preserve the foundations of freedom and liberty for all future generations. The American people would not take "no" for an answer. But would they finish the task they had undertaken in the general election?

Trump: the Unlikely Leader

CHAPTER XI

A s you well understand by now, this book is not about any one individual, but rather about a movement taking place across America in the name of one individual, Donald Trump. In all likelihood, no one was more shocked by what was happening in the 2016 election cycle than that man himself.

Throughout his life, Trump was focused entirely upon building a successful family business that would eventually reach levels of success seldom seen, even in the land of the free and home of the brave, where all things were once possible and anyone could achieve his goals. Known as a tough, highly intelligent, very focused and driven, sometimes brash and even over-the-top self-promoter, Trump had built not only a dynasty, but also a worldwide public persona that would earn him the admiration of many, and the bitter hate, disdain and envy of others not so impressed by his hard work and sacrifices.

Almost 34 years ago, in a 1988 interview with Oprah Winfrey,

Trump was asked if he would ever consider running for President, as he criticized foreign trade policies. Trump said he "was sick of watching America lose," and although he had never considered running for high office at the time, he "would never rule it out." The young Trump said he would consider setting his life's ambition and work aside if he felt that the country needed him and he could help.

For years now, many have stated many times that the people best suited to run this country never seem to run for office. They are people with real accomplishments under their belts, executive experience, successful track records of leadership, skin in the game and a reason to defend the foundations of freedom and liberty that made it possible for them to achieve what they had.

At the beginning of our nation, 240 years ago, our Founding Fathers thought it wise to limit voting to landowners only. It's one of many sound ideas that has since been tossed away. Despite the "politically incorrect" nature of such an idea today, there is sound reasoning behind it. The concept was simply based upon the principle that the decisions of a government of, by and for the people should be made by those who had a stake in the game and who had demonstrated the ability to lead their own lives successfully before they should be allowed to lead a country.

Today, we're all too familiar with the likes of Harry Reid, Bill and Hillary Clinton and Barack and Michelle Obama, who entered public office essentially dead broke and somehow became multi-millionaires on government salaries.[1] Rarely, though, does anyone who has gained major success in the private sector choose to become a public servant. Is Donald Trump an unlikely leader of the people's revolt, circa 2016? The answer is both yes and no.

For decades, the American people had been seeking a hero to rise up and lead the nation out of darkness and into the light. They yearned for someone who could demonstrate concrete achievements, who had a stake in the game and a reason to protect and preserve the foundations of freedom and liberty for all. They wanted someone who was not a career politician but rather a political outsider who still connects with America — and Americans — up close and personal.

As personal qualifications go, Trump is not at all unlikely. He has a resume crammed with executive achievement. The unlikely part of the equation is the likelihood that someone with his accomplishments and (let's face it) his luxurious lifestyle would set his personal interests aside to seek the dangerous and thankless job of President of the United States of America.

As of the 113th Congress, that governmental body is the wealthiest club in America. More than half of the members of Congress are millionaires. This fact alone is not a negative until you realize how many of these supposed public servants gained their wealth as a result of their public office, and how many of them own private sector businesses that hold government contracts. These men and women control the manipulation of the markets as their "private portfolios" ride that roller coaster — affording members of Congress, their families and friends, the highest rates of return on earth.

The people had allowed public office to become the biggest get-rich-quick Ponzi scheme in the country. It's a level of governmental corruption and theft that makes Bernie Madoff look like a Boy

Scout. As these "public servants" enrich themselves and bail out the "too big to fail" banks that line their pockets, they drive the people deeper and deeper into debt and poverty. The politicians were too big to fail— at least in their minds.

So the idea that a private sector billionaire like Donald Trump presents some form of threat to the average American is just plain nutty. It is the D.C. millionaires club that has driven the nation to the brink of extinction, and every American into a socio-economic corner. While Trump talks about "making America great again," his establishment opponents worry only about how to continue making themselves rich!

Many of Trump's critics have raised concerns over Trump's "lack of experience" or "expertise" in governmental affairs. It's a fair question for any candidate from outside the political establishment. But most of these critics are the very "experts" who have driven our nation into ruin. It is "legal experts" who are most responsible for undermining natural law rights and constitutional justice by way of Marxist "social justice." It is "economic experts" who ran up $20 trillion in national debt with over another $120 trillion in unfunded liabilities. It is "foreign policy experts" who toppled the sovereign governments of numerous Middle Eastern countries, creating a vacuum now filled by Islamic terrorist organizations, also funded, trained and aided by Obama administration officials, all of them so-called "experts."

In 2016, 16 primary challengers worked together in an effort to prevent Donald Trump from becoming the GOP nominee. All of them were either establishment insiders like Jeb Bush, Marco Rubio and John Kasich, or cohorts of establishment insiders like

Cruz, Fiorina and Walker. One by one, they were all eliminated from the race — not by Trump — but by American voters who had lost all faith in any D.C. insider. (NOTE: *denotes insider; **denotes ineligible insider.*)

THE 2016 GOP PRIMARY CHALLENGERS

1. Donald Trump .... (presumed GOP nominee)
2. *John Kasich .... (withdrew May 4)
3. **Ted Cruz .... (withdrew May 3)
4. **Marco Rubio .... (withdrew March 15)
5. Ben Carson .... (withdrew March 2)
6. *Jeb Bush .... (withdrew Feb 20)
7. *Jim Gilmore .... (withdrew Feb 12)
8. *Chris Christie .... (withdrew Feb 10)
9. *Carly Fiorina .... (withdrew Feb 10)
10. *Rick Santorum .... (withdrew Feb 3)
11. *Rand Paul .... (withdrew Feb 3)
12. *Mike Huckabee .... (withdrew Feb *1*)
13. *George Pataki .... (withdrew Dec 29)
14. *Lindsey Graham .... (withdrew Dec 21)
15. **Bobby Jindal .... (withdrew Nov 17)
16. *Scott Walker .... (withdrew Sept 21)
17. *Rick Perry .... (withdrew Sept 11)

Of the original 17 GOP candidates, three were constitutionally ineligible under Article II of the U.S. Constitution: Cruz, Rubio and Jindal. All were recognized RNC insiders except for three: Trump, Carson and Fiorina.

The real story of who created the Trump revolution is not just about the organic uprising of *the silent majority* fueling the Trump campaign to the nomination by May 2016. Another critical part of the story dates back to early 2015, when Republican Party elites had unwittingly Trumped themselves.

In February 2015, before anyone had officially entered the GOP primary race, Republican Party elites had already chosen Jeb Bush as their preferred 2016 nominee. All they had to do was manipulate the early primaries to position him for the win.

At the time however, Wisconsin Governor Scott Walker was the people's choice. He led the prospect field with 47% of GOP voter support among conservative voters, compared to Cruz running second at 11% and Trump and Carson at the back of the pack around 1%, according to Drudge Report polling data from nearly a half-million very conservative-leaning subscribers.[2]

While Walker was a GOP insider, he was not yet playing ball with the D.C. establishment. In fact, his state-level battles with public sector labor unions had given D.C. insiders heartburn over Walker's national office prospects, even though he had won those battles with labor unions, three times in a row.

In order to advance a Bush nomination, the powers that be had to push Walker out of front runner status quickly, before the people had a chance to unify behind him in the more conservative state primaries. So Walker became the first casualty of the Republican Party machine intent upon forcing Jeb Bush onto the 2016 ticket. After a concentrated assault on Walker by his own party machinery, he fell like a rock from 47% in February 2015 to 1% in September. He dropped out of the race on September 21.

Party elites thought they had just cleared the path for Jeb, believing that Trump did not have the staying power to finish the race, much less win the nomination. Despite hovering at the 5% mark for months, Jeb Bush remained in the race, thanks to a huge campaign fund, awaiting the moment when Trump would stumble and fall — and Jeb could slide into the "lesser of two evils" position formerly occupied by Mitt Romney in 2012 and John McCain in 2008.

What the party elites had overlooked in their "expert" analysis and strategic planning was the people in the voting booth. They had had enough of party elite manipulations of the election process and were looking to make some changes of their own in 2016.

The elites also overlooked the fact that an unconstitutional usurper in our White House, Barack Hussein Obama, had forced Americans to return to their Founding documents in search of how to regain control of their constitutional republic from foreign interests. In that process, they learned what the Article II requirements for office really are — and that aside from extending the Article II requirements for president to the office of vice president in Amendment XII, these stipulations have never changed.

The *natural born Citizen* requirement remains intact, despite eight separate congressional attempts to eliminate it statutorily and seven years of effort to end it via Obama precedence.[3] After being forced to relearn the foundations of freedom and liberty with a renewed interest in the U.S. Constitution, the people now knew that Obama, Cruz, Rubio and Jindal were all constitutionally ineligible to occupy the Oval Office.

Once Scott Walker was forced out of the race to make room for Jeb Bush — Cruz, Rubio and Jindal never had any real chance in the GOP primaries. A growing number of conservative voters had learned from the Obama administration what the Founders meant by *natural born Citizen* and why (to prevent foreign occupation and rule), that status exists as a requirement for the Oval Office.

Long-term RNC insiders like Graham, Pataki, Bush, Santorum and Kasich also had no real chance of gaining the support of grassroots GOP voters in 2016. All of them were seen as part of the problem and therefore incapable of delivering any real solutions to America's plight.

Once the RNC shot itself in the foot by eliminating Walker from the race, they had already *trumped* themselves in the GOP primaries. Trump was the only person left in the race who was not a D.C. insider, constitutionally ineligible, or a fringe candidate with nothing on his resume worthy of support.

The RNC elites *trumped* themselves. In their effort to outsmart the electorate and control the outcome of the GOP primaries, they defeated themselves. They created the anger in their own constituency that would soon become a nationwide revolt against the Washington establishment. They created the monster they now feared.

As the campaigns headed into New York, it was clear that no one except Trump had a pathway to the GOP nomination. The only hope for RNC establishment types was to force a contested convention by using Cruz and Kasich to win just enough delegates to prevent Trump from hitting the magic number of 1,237 delegates he needed to win the nomination on the first ballot at the GOP convention in Cleveland.

In the days that followed, even those establishment hopes would be dashed as Trump swept state after state with widening margins: New York 60.4% of the vote, Connecticut 57.9%, Delaware 60.8%, Maryland 54.4%, Pennsylvania 56.7% and Rhode Island 63.8%. That left only Indiana as the last opportunity for RNC elites to block the Trump revolution. But he won 53.3% of the vote in Indiana. At this point, no one was even close to challenging Trump.

It turned out that the more RNC establishment elites worked to derail the Trump revolution, the more strength it gained. Eventually, GOP voters left no doubt in anyone's mind that they were determined to take back control of their party — and Washington.

Is Trump the right man to lead this revolt and make America great again? Only time will tell. But one thing is very clear: The American people have bet the future of their nation on Donald Trump, categorically rejecting every other contender.

It should shock no one that many establishment insiders are having great difficulty gathering the courage and decency to unify behind their own party's nominee. As a highly contentious and often vicious primary process draws to a close, both parties must face the reality that, barring unforeseen events, either Trump, Clinton or Sanders will be the next President of the United States. Many who were pitted against one another throughout the primary process will need some time to collect themselves and look forward from here, letting go of their defeats and focusing on the future.

Trump can help the reconciliation process by holding the ground he took in order to gain the trust of American voters, while reaching out to bring others aboard without compromising the principles and values that made him the nominee. His choice of running mate will be critical in this endeavor.

Trump will not be able to hold his primary supporters by choosing any D.C. insider or even worse, one of his constitutionally ineligible primary opponents as his running mate. Cruz, Rubio and Jindal must be off the table. Insiders like Bush, Kasich, Walker, Romney, Ryan and Graham must also be off the table.

To hold and build upon the momentum he has from the primaries, Trump will have to hold true to his principles and commitments to all voters who placed their trust in him. A misstep in choosing a running mate could be catastrophic to everything he and his supporters worked so hard to build.

As we have stated several times throughout this book, this is not an endorsement of Trump. Nor is it an effort to advise him on his choice of running mate or cabinet members. But the writing is on the wall. The people behind the Trump revolution are in no mood for any form of compromise. They have chosen Trump in part, because they are sick and tired of watching their principles and values compromised away by D.C. Republicans who have totally failed to stop the Obama administration from destroying our country, or hold anyone in it accountable for their many misdeeds.

The process of picking a winning running mate must begin with the elimination of everyone who could lose Trump some of his current support. That pretty much eliminates all of Trump's primary opponents, especially those who are constitutionally ineligible.

The people fueling the Trump revolution are not interested in compromise. They are not interested in unconstitutional running mates or D.C. insiders whom they would love to see on the unemployment line after November.

The people want Trump to finish the task they started, without exception, without compromise and without apology. They want their party and their country back—and they do not intend to accept anything less.

TRUMPED by the People
CHAPTER XII

It wasn't the individual who was setting the American political world on its head. Millions of disgusted Americans at the foundation of the "Trump phenomenon" were responsible for teaching party establishment insiders and their complicit main stream media machine a lesson in what *the people* are really capable of, once they lose all faith and trust in those they elected to handle national affairs.

Trump himself is a formidable foe or ally, to be certain. But alone, no one person can cause the political tsunami rushing from sea to shining sea, from every race, creed, color, past political affiliation and socio-economic standing. No, what was happening in 2016 had very little to do with the man called Trump, and everything to do with the people who were showing up in record numbers to make certain that Trump was the man chosen to lead our country back to the greatness our Founders and forefathers intended for all posterity.

In a rush to catch up with Trump supporters and understand their motives, the RNC and their corporate media ran survey after survey trying to figure out who the Trump supporter really is. They failed in that effort because of an ideological blindness that simply would not allow them to see the truth right under their noses.

Who are these "Trumpsters?" The answer can be summed up in three words: *the silent majority.* They are average Americans who normally are quiet objectors to the obvious demise of a once great country. They get up every day and go to work, feed and house their families, raise their kids and look after Grandma and Grandpa. They normally keep their noses to the grindstone believing that somehow all of the political nonsense will work itself out.

Since 2008, *the silent majority* had become much more vocal, but their voices were being ignored. The number one common factor among Trump supporters and even voters in general in 2016, is that they are being ignored. No matter how loud they scream at elected officials after each election, no one pays attention. No matter which political party they entrust with power, the end result is the same: the ongoing demise of their country.

This reality not only accounts for the GOP upset wherein Trump out-performed all 16 other GOP candidates, but also why Hillary Clinton is struggling to defeat Bernie Sanders in the Democrat primaries, as well as why she will likely be in no position to successfully unify Democrat voters come November.

As for the Trump supporters, women represent 50.8% of the U.S. population today, about the same percentage of women supporting Trump. Fifty percent of Trump supporters are between the ages of 45 and 65, with another 34% over age 65. Most are average per-capita income folks, middle class Americans, although an estimated 11% of Trump supporters earn $100,000 per year or more. Twenty percent identify themselves as "liberal" or "moderate" voters, while 65% identify themselves as "conservative," with another 13% identifying as "very conservative." Fewer than one-third of all Trump supporters claim any affiliation with the Tea Party. *(According to Real Clear Politics polling data.)*

Studies of the GOP primaries showed Trump taking voters from every GOP candidate except Jeb Bush. Although Trump started at the back of the pack in 2015, other candidates failed to catch fire, or steadily lost their support base through the primary season. Finally, all were forced to drop out of the race as the political winds continued to blow in Trump's direction. In part, the overt Republican Party efforts to derail Trump seemed to cause voters to shift to him more and more. In essence, the movement was a mass revolt against establishment insider efforts to control the outcome of the primary process, against the will of the vast majority of GOP voters.

RNC media shills continued to claim that Trump "would never be able to defeat Hillary Clinton" in the November general elections. However, Clinton had her own problems and was narrowly hanging on to her lead in the Democratic Party race with only one challenger: card-carrying socialist Bernie Sanders, who had no history of executive experience or personal accomplishment on his resume. The Clinton War Machine that lost the 2008 nomination to Barack Obama was in no condition to sweep the DNC nomination in 2016. Without their "super-delegates," Clinton might even be losing to Bernie Sanders.

So the idea that Trump, who had defeated 16 GOP primary challengers and taken the GOP nomination by storm, would somehow lack the power to defeat Clinton, who was barely beating Sanders, was disingenuous, to say the least. These push-poll driven headlines were just additional media propaganda efforts intended to drive support away from Trump and toward either an RNC insider, Bush, or a Tea Party darling, like Cruz or Rubio.

It was the average American who was TRUMPING the system in 2016, openly rejecting all D.C. establishment insiders, including prior Tea Party favorites such as Cruz and Rubio, who had also failed the people in Congress. The people were searching for someone who they believed would totally upset the apple cart. These voters were looking for a political outsider as fed up with establishment do-nothings as they were. And they believed that this person was Donald Trump.

What do *the people* want in 2016? The same things they wanted in 2010, when voters swept Democrats from the House and placed the House of Representatives under the command and control of Republicans — many of them Tea Party candidates who have failed to use their power to stop, or even slow Obama's destruction of the good ole' USA. The same things they tried to accomplish in 2014, when they voted Republicans into control of the U.S. Senate, only to be once again ignored by those they had just elected into power.

Now convinced that no one in the Republican-controlled Congress was ever going to stand up for them, or hold anyone accountable for anything including acts of tyranny, treachery and treason from both the executive and judicial branches of government, *the silent majority* was done chattering amongst themselves. And they were ready to bet the farm on a billionaire business mogul from New York, who was saying what most Americans had been feeling and thinking for years: that our country is in dire condition, on code-blue status, gasping its last breath, in desperate need of a full-scale constitutional revival and resuscitation that only a D.C. outsider would ever dare attempt.

The people behind the Trump tsunami are responsible for the nationwide revolt against inside the Beltway anti-Americanism. That includes both the "anti-imperialist" counter-revolution currently in command of all national assets (and governmental agencies) under Obama Democrats and the do-nothing Republicans who are either on-board the Obama train headed for the cliff, or too cowardly to stand up against it.

But *the people* would have help from an unexpected quarter who was openly opposed to the revolt. In the end, the RNC powers would assist in the hostile takeover of their party by D.C. outsiders. The harder they worked in the open to derail any candidate who might have challenged the status quo in D.C., the angrier the voters became, and the more they shifted to Trump in response to overt inner-party attempts to overrule the will of the voters. The same thing was happening in the Democratic Party as Sanders supporters sought to derail Clinton for much the same reason.

In the end, even other GOP candidates like Cruz and Kasich, who were working with RNC powers in a failed attempt to block Trump from reaching the needed 1,237 delegates by staying in the race well beyond any reasonable point, would pay a price for their actions. People once supportive of their campaigns turned on those candidates, disgusted by the elite's public display of animosity towards their voters. In many cases, Cruz, Kasich and their cohorts characterized Trump supporters as "low-information voters, stupid, uneducated and racist." They alienated millions — in fact a vast majority of GOP voters — by parroting leftist character assaults aimed not only at Trump but also his supporters.

No doubt the 2016 election cycle will be recorded in history as a moment when *the people* had had enough of Washington politics and the self-absorbed, self-serving and power-hungry D.C. insiders were given their walking papers. It wasn't as much about who the people wanted to put in power as it was about who they wanted to remove from power.

To some degree, *the people* were simply looking for a RESET button to push. They had lost all faith and confidence in all three branches of their federal government, all of which had become destructive of their only purpose for existence: to secure the inalienable natural rights of all legal American citizens and at all times provide for the common defense thereof. That's not all though.

The people had also lost all faith and confidence in the election system itself. It was not just due to visible signs of voter fraud, vote tampering, voting rights being extended to illegal aliens and felons, or the massive influence of foreign money in U.S. political campaigns, but it was also due to delegate wrangling by the two political parties. A number of things have to be fixed in the U.S. election system itself before *the people* will regain any confidence in that system:

WHAT NEEDS TO CHANGE IN AMERICAN ELECTIONS

1. The GOP should do away with all "open primaries" wherein liberals, Democrats and independents of all political ideologies can engage in the selection of GOP nominees. Open primaries are akin to allowing wolves to

vote in a sheep's primary for which a wolf would become the leader of the sheep in order to lead them to slaughter.

2. There should never be any "undeclared" delegates on any GOP ballot. Casting a ballot for any "undeclared" delegate is equal to passing your vote off to someone else to do with as they please.

3. All candidates must be properly vetted and certified as "eligible for the office" they are seeking, by the Secretary of State, who also serves as the state's Chief Elections Officer. We cannot rely on the political parties to properly vet their own, as demonstrated by the DNC with Barack Obama and the RNC with Cruz, Rubio and Jindal.

4. There should be no "motor-voter" laws allowing people to register as voters and vote on the same day. In the past few elections, people were able to vote in multiple districts and even in more than one state by simply being bused from one district to another and using "motor-voter" statutes to cast ballots on the same day they registered, using false residency on their registration forms. *(Worst of all, churches were often used to accomplish this overt election fraud, as well as that of illegal immigrant voting, as reported in several election cycles — predominately in northern Ohio.)*

5. Republican Party primaries should not begin in the most liberal states of the country. Under this arrangement, the most conservative candidates are likely to be eliminated from the race before a conservative-leaning state even has an opportunity to vote.

6. Voting machines should produce a paper receipt for each voter, as confirmation and proof of proper vote registering and counting. Machines for the GOP should not be under the servicing of left-leaning contractors who have access to the software setup in those machines. The opportunity and temptation to play games with the machines and manipulate the outcome of elections is just too great.

More than anything else, the 2016 election cycle is an attempt by the people, most of them behind Trump, to retake control of the GOP and the country and restore some semblance of honor, decency, truth and constitutional protections for the people at large. It isn't only conservative Republican voters who want America to be great again. People of all political persuasions know that America is in deep trouble right now. Voters from all walks of life and all past political alliances are banding together in the Trump movement to restore some form of sanity in American politics. All of these people want to regain at least some sense of confidence in the system built to provide *self-governance* to everyone.

The 2016 election is about much more than one man. The movement behind Trump is less driven by that individual than by all of the factors that make him attractive to millions of angry American voters who are tired of being treated like they don't matter.

The people are sick of being treated like mindless fools, bought off with a pittance in federal handouts in exchange for their individual freedom and liberty. The people want to control their own destiny in America again and end the era of big government tyranny from the three branches, all of which have become the greatest threat to American sovereignty, security, liberty and prosperity.

Many in the "political expert" class who have run this nation aground will continue to question and doubt the logic fueling the Trump revolution. But one thing they can doubt no longer is the depth of commitment in *the people.* They clearly intend to force pro-American change in America, via the Trump revolution. The resolve among Trump supporters has not been seen in this country since voters from across the political spectrum gathered together to replace Jimmy Carter with Ronald Reagan.

Like it or not, understand it or not, *the silent majority* is speaking!

Issues Fueling the Trump Train
CHAPTER XIII

I n every election cycle, candidates, their political spin-doctors, news journalists and pundits claim to want to focus on "the issues" affecting the elections. Yet they seldom want to confront the actual issues that drive voters at the polls. Instead, they prefer to dictate to voters which issues they should be focused upon, of course, in order to control public sentiments and voting patterns to deliver the predetermined outcome as established by, guess who — the establishment.

In reality, the people telling us which issues we should care about most, only care about maintaining their own power positions and keeping their own money train on track, as they choke the life out of the goose that laid the golden egg responsible for a once-great nation.

Voters below age 40 probably don't realize that for more than 30 years now, the number one issue on the minds of every American voter is "the economy," jobs! Which means, for the past 30 years or more, despite every election being based on economic improvement in the minds of every voter, no one elected in the past 30 years has ever solved the economic crisis in our country, no matter which political party is in charge in any of the three branches of the federal government.

Election after election for more than 30 years was supposed to solve our economic crisis. Thirty years later, the only economic improvement in America is in the personal pockets of the people we elected to solve our economic woes.

Meanwhile, the candidates, their experts and pundits tell us that we are more concerned with a laundry list of special interest single issues from global warming to transgender rights, black lives matter, a woman's right to kill her young before they even get a chance at life and partisan bickering. It's akin to keeping your eye on a sleight-of-hand artist: While the magician keeps your attention focused on his right hand, the left hand is doing all the dirty work and when the trick is over, the average onlooker is dumbfounded and amazed. They were watching the wrong hand.

Politics works the same way. The "experts" hold your attention on their right hand, while their left hand does all of the dirty work. Their minions in the media provide the backdrop and shift your attention from ring to ring as the circus band plays on. As a result, people who often properly identify the issue or issues of greatest importance, somehow fail to connect the dots in order to achieve their intended objectives in every election. They take their eye off the ball just long enough to miss the secret to the trick.

In poll after poll, election after election, the number one issue for most American voters has been "it's the economy stupid." Yet, year after year, election after election, that issue goes unresolved no matter the outcome of the election. Why?

The answer is this: Although the people have correctly identified the biggest problem, "the economy stupid," they usually fail to connect all of the dots in order to understand what is causing their economic crisis or how to fix it. Before the people can solve the economic problems in America, they must connect all of the related dots responsible for the crisis and then address those issues accordingly.

As an example, sadly, although many Americans are familiar with the term U.S. Constitution, a much smaller number have ever read that document or — if they have — understand what it means. Few today can accurately tell you the difference between the U.S. Constitution and the Bill of Rights. Yet, many will refer to both as "their rights" when in fact, both are "constitutional protections" of our "inalienable natural rights" that were "endowed by our Creator" and exist beyond the legal authority of any man.

During public appearances, I often ask attendees, "How many Amendments are in the Bill of Rights?" In the circles I travel, most will correctly answer, ten. Then I state, "Nine of those 10 Amendments are entirely dependent upon one. Which one?" I can watch the minds go blank in the room at this point, in most cases. People seldom step back and think, connect the dots, or make sure that their next decision is a sound decision before making it.

The answer is that nine of the 10 Amendments in the Bill of Rights are entirely dependent upon the Second Amendment. The inalienable right of the people to "keep and bear arms" is what gives the people the power to protect all other rights. Without the Second Amendment, the people can protect and enforce no other rights. Of course, this explains why the federal government and the world at large, is so focused upon stripping every American of his Second Amendment rights. If the government is ever allowed to infringe upon the Second Amendment, every Amendment and constitutional protection of our natural rights will vanish with it. In fact, every natural right of every American citizen depends entirely upon this one right to keep and bear arms. Without it, Americans can defend and enforce no other rights whatsoever.

Likewise, when looking at the issues fueling the Trump revolution today, again, "the economy stupid" ranks number one among voters who have voted on this basis for decades now, without ever solving the problem. In just the past seven years, the Obama administration has doubled our national debt, from $10 trillion upon taking office to over $20 trillion by the time he leaves office, with an additional $120 trillion in "unfunded liabilities" that our elected officials have saddled every legal American citizen with for generations to come.

Meanwhile, the American "middle class" has been forced out of existence, jobs have been lost by the millions, the dollar is on the verge of total collapse and our elected "experts" talk about balancing the federal budget 25 years from now. I guess they missed the "it's the economy, stupid" message altogether, on both sides of the aisle.

During a recent campaign speech, the morally and ethically bankrupt Hillary Clinton asked the crowd at a campaign stop, "What's Trump going to do, bankrupt the country the same way he bankrupted two of his casinos?" It's one of Hillary's better ideas, actually.

It was Bill, Hillary, Bernie, Obama and all of their "expert" friends who bankrupted our country long before Trump ever considered seeking public office. But Trump may in fact be the right person to steer our nation through the bankruptcy created by the past crop of "experts" in D.C. who drove our country into the economic toilet. Maybe Trump is the only man able to lead our country through bankruptcy and out the other side in better shape.

Back to connecting the right dots…

Like many elections before, the 2016 election cycle is once again all "about the economy, stupid." But this time, the people are starting to connect some of the dots they must connect in order to address this issue. Trump recently said, "only a rich nation is a powerful nation," and he is right about that. Throughout our history, America's supremacy (or as the leftists call it, imperialism) in the world was the direct result of our productivity and wealth as a free people. In order to return our nation to that *shining city on the hill,* we must end the bankrupting of our nation, which must begin with ending the economic assault on the American people.

Public polling data coming into the 2016 election cycle lists the following items as most important among a broad range of American voters:[1]

KEY PRIORITIES OF THE 2016 ELECTION

1. The Economy and Jobs
2. Terrorism/Foreign Policy
3. Federal deficit and budget
4. Wall Street/Equality
5. Health Care
6. Immigration
7. Environment and Global Warming
8. Guns

NOTE: *We intentionally chose an NBC News poll because it included a cross section of Republican, Democrat and independent voters and may indeed represent a broad view of average American voters, as opposed to pollsters commonly known to slant more to one political side or another. However, in reviewing a number of other polls, they all trended very similarly.*

Once again, voters name the economy and jobs as priority issue number one in the 2016 elections. In this case, they name terrorism and foreign policy second and essentially, out of control federal spending third, all three of which are actually directly associated with the health and well-being of the U.S. (or any other) economy. This confirms our earlier notion that the people are beginning to properly connect some critical dots.

Notice that gun rights appears at number eight on the list of critical issues, which indicates that the people are not yet connecting the dots between gun rights and every other natural right protected by our Constitution. However, a more in-depth look behind this issue demonstrates a very clear view that in general, Republicans support Second Amendment rights and Democrats support advancing efforts at gun control, by a wide margin. In other words, this is a highly partisan issue that widely separates the views of the two voting groups.

Just above guns on the list is the environment and global warming, which again is a highly partisan issue. Most Republicans believe it is globalist-driven voodoo science while most Democrat voters believe that the sky is falling simply because Al Gore said so. However, the mere fact that this issue appears at number seven on the list is an indication that even most Democrats have not bought into the *Chicken Little* global warming theory, or at least, are intelligent enough to know that we must save humans before saving trees.

However, regarding the next item at number six on the survey results, immigration, which once again fails to distinguish "legal immigration" from "illegal invasion," treating both as one in the same subject, when in reality they are two entirely separate issues. The people fail to connect the critical dots between mass *illegal migration* or *invasion* and American jobs lost, increased federal welfare and *social justice* spending, additional related *unfunded liabilities,* new threats to national security and a total collapse of national sovereignty, all of which negatively and directly impacts our economy, listed at priority number one.[2]

Item number six, immigration, is actually directly associated with items 1, 2, 3, 5 and 8 on the list. Because the federal government is currently granting "illegal migrants" more rights than legal American citizens, the mass migration of illegal aliens into the USA has a direct negative impact on the U.S. economy, jobs for American citizens, terrorism, foreign policy, national security and sovereignty, health care, gun rights, the federal budget and our exploding national debt. In fact, the ongoing illegal invasion of our nation may in reality, represent the single largest threat to every priority listed on the survey results. Still, the people placed its level of importance at number six on the list.

The federal government is violating existing U.S. immigration and naturalization laws, essentially refusing to faithfully execute those laws as required by every oath of public office, allowing millions of illegal aliens to enter and remain in the USA taking U.S. jobs from American citizens in search of work. In addition, an estimated 2.8 million American jobs have been exported overseas on Obama's watch.

The result of these insane policies has been record U.S. unemployment. According to the Obama administration using the U3 method, it is 5.2%, but according to real numbers using the U6 method, it is 23%. To put this in proper perspective, the rates of unemployment before Obama took office in 2008 were 5% (U3) and 9.2% (U6). Seven years into the Obama administration, unemployment remains at or worse than that of the Bush administration. Note that in both cases, the U3 method of calculating the unemployment rate only accounts for 54% of the actual jobless rate, which is responsible for the difference between U3 and U6 reports.[3]

NOTE: *Both U3 and U6 are different mathematical formulas for calculating and reporting to the public, the performance of governmental policies. U3 only tells a piece of the overall picture, whereas U6 presents a more complete accounting of reality.*

Under-employment, which describes the condition of Americans unable to find work in their chosen professions and forced to take a lesser job at lesser pay to feed their families, often working more than one job to make ends meet, is at or above 30% of the current workforce.[4] In addition, by the 2016 elections, stagnated wages, a record loss of private U.S. wealth and deteriorating economic conditions left the average American unable to financially manage even a $1,000 unexpected family crisis. By standard economic indicators, the U.S. economy has remained dead level with no real growth since January 2009, as our national debt doubled during the same period.

What the current leaders in D.C. have proven is that we cannot borrow our way out of debt as a nation. They have also proven that the more the federal government gets involved in private sector business, refuses to faithfully execute our immigration laws and allows our country to be overtaken by illegal migration, the more economic calamity we find ourselves in as a people and a nation.

So, the fact that the people continue to miss the direct connections between immigration policies and their jobs is highly troubling. There is no way to fix one without first fixing the other and it has nothing to do with racism or any general dislike for "legal" immigration. It has to do with shipping U.S. jobs overseas while importing *illegal foreign workers* to take American jobs from American citizens, many illegally receiving federal benefits on American soil.

Trump is resonating with American voters across all past partisan lines, largely due to the single issue of *illegal* immigration, which no other candidate from either political party is willing to directly address even today. The average American voter is simply sick and tired of playing second fiddle to illegal migrants in their own country, losing their wealth, earnings, security and future just so that D.C. politicians can pander to the "illegal alien" vote, when people in the United States illegally are not even legally allowed to vote. The truth is after the political "experts" in D.C. destroyed the American middle class, they sought to import a new middle class via *illegal* immigration, with the full intent of granting amnesty to all of them once they have too many here to deport (aka, too big to fail), and make them new American taxpayers to replace the American taxpayers they had driven into bankruptcy.

Whether Trump builds a wall or not, or can force Mexico to pay for that wall, both of which are easily accomplished if desired, his message regarding "putting America (and Americans) first" is resonating with millions of American voters regardless of their past political affiliations. The distinction between the average American politician and Trump appears to be that Trump recognizes the reality that no one can "make America great again" without making "Americans" great again. Trump is connecting the dots that the people have had trouble connecting of late.

Then we come to item number four, the issue of so-called Wall Street equality. From K-12 and on every U.S. college campus today, unionized teachers and 60s anti-imperialist professors, along with their media friends, have convinced millions of Americans that capitalism is evil, greedy and bad for America, despite free market capitalism creating the most productive, prosperous and powerful nation ever known to mankind. So, it should shock no one that an assault on Wall Street ranks number four on an NBC (or any other mainstream media) survey today. The anti-American indoctrination has been very effective over the past hundred years or so.

But in reality again, Wall Street is for "investors." Investors, include not only every Wall Street high roller, but millions of American retirees and workers with an IRA or 401k today, all of whom are investing in their own futures by investing in yours. Investors provide private capital to private sector businesses and industry, which in turn, use those resources to hire new employees (jobs) and expand operations with new inventions, innovations, products, services and in general, economic growth.

Therefore, it is not possible to restrict the potential for return on investment on Wall Street without also restricting job creation, productivity, innovation and economic growth. In fact, if you study the productivity, economic growth and private wealth on a state-by-state basis, you will easily learn that governments cannot create jobs or private wealth. Governments can only get in the way, or out of the way of the private sector. Governments can only create government (aka, taxpayer funded) jobs. Pro-business states far out-perform anti-business states without exception. Anti-business states governed by anti-imperialist Democrats are all bankrupt and heavily dependent upon the rest of the country for their very existence. But conservative-run (usually Republican) pro-economic growth states, are as a rule, in far better economic condition.

In a free market economy, "sharing the wealth" takes the form of economic growth wherein all who participate in that growth benefit from it. But in a progressive Marxist economy, the government decides how much is too much for some, in order to decide how much is too little for others. These concepts fail repeatedly the world over because they remove from society any motivation or incentive for productivity and reward both producer and non-producer equally, regardless of unequal output or participation.

That brings the discussion to item number five, health care. America's venture into government-run socialized medicine, lovingly referred to as Obamacare, has already proven to be a total failure by any estimation, by any honest analysis. When Democrat friends at Harvard and National Public Radio (NPR) declare Obamacare "a total failure," you know your famed enterprise is going down in flames.

National Public Radio collaborated with Harvard's T.H. Chan School of Public Health and the Robert Wood Johnson Foundation to survey Americans' recent experience with health care. As to the

Affordable Care Act, the survey's findings are damning. They suggest that Obamacare has been worse than a complete waste of money. (Powerline, March 2016) [5]

The simple truth is that nothing on this earth is free, certainly not health care. The people who voted for Democrats to usher in socialized medicine did so believing they would receive health care for "free" or at the minimum, for much less than they were previously spending. But as with everything the government runs, Obamacare was doomed from the start — designed, organized, passed in the dead of night along purely partisan lines and implemented by people who know absolutely nothing at all about health care — namely politicians.

The staff of Sen. Jeff Sessions (R-Ala.) spent three months combing through the hundreds of pages of the law and comparing their expected costs to the United States fiscal outlook for the next 75 years — just as the government currently does for other programs such as Social Security and Medicare. Sen. Sessions said, "I was floored by what we discovered." And well he should have been: His staff estimated that Obamacare had created an additional $17 trillion *unfunded liability* for the U.S. government.

How did the government do with running the Veterans Administration? If you are a veteran, or have one in the family, you know the answer to this question. How did the government do at running Social Security, other than bleeding it dry for unintended and illegal social experiments? We are $20 trillion in debt folks. How is your government doing at running anything?

Listen up! Stop calling it "federal debt" and "federal deficits." The federal government has no debt at all. The American people are on the hook for every penny their government spends and every penny it runs up in debt, plus interest. This debt is being created by our federal government, but every penny of that debt is owed by the American citizens, not the federal government or the individuals running it into the ground. WAKE UP!

NOTE: *When you add our current $20 trillion in debt to the additional estimated $120 trillion in future unfunded liabilities committed to by the Obama administration, American citizens currently have a total government debt liability of at least $140 trillion. If you divide that federal liability by an estimated 320 million American citizens, counting all men, women and children of all ages today, each American currently owes $437,500 plus interest, as his or her "fair share" of the debt created by our federal representatives. Because the federal government is bankrupt, every American who owes that debt is also bankrupt, whether or not they know it yet. What percentage of Americans could pay their $437,500 bill today? Every American child born today is born with a $437,500 debt.*

If the economy and jobs really are the most important issues in this or any other election, and they should be, then the American people must connect all of these dots and address all of these issues or they will never be able to improve their economic future.

There is no way to borrow our way out of debt. There is no way to improve the U.S. economy via government actions, other than the government stepping out of the way entirely and letting the American people do what they do best: produce. We will never have a bustling economy when our country is overrun by illegal aliens and jihadists. The government has bankrupted every program it has ever run and should never be trusted with life and death decisions over their citizens through government-run health care of any type, under any design.

Trump appears to be connecting most if not all of these dots, which is why he is resonating with millions of Americans who are also able to connect at least some of the dots. When all Americans can connect all of these dots, they will reclaim the national glory of their past.

2016 is absolutely an issues-driven election. But it isn't the usual divisive special-interest-issue election. It is a unifying issues election wherein the focus is on the fundamentals of good self-governance and the all-American desire for our country to become great again!

Is 2016 the Turning Point?

CHAPTER XIV

For the past 240 years, America's history has been written as it was unfolding. The story of *the 2016 turning point,* the New American Revolution unfolding today under the political banner TRUMP, continues to unfold as this book is written and released.

As a people, we have gone from the first revolution to win our independence to the anti-American counter-revolution aiming to destroy the United States and "fundamentally transform America" into a third world member of a global commune. Now we are moving to the era of a second American revolution in which the people are reclaiming control of their political system. Throughout those nearly two and a half centuries, America, like life itself, has been in a constant state of change.

As this chapter is being written, students are graduating from high school and college with their eyes fixed on their future, as radical 60s counter-revolutionaries give "scholarly" commencement speeches to wide-eyed youths searching for any reason to hope. Secretary of State John Kerry recently stood before a full arena at Northeastern University and told the graduates to "prepare for a borderless world" as he spoon-fed Marxist globalization pabulum to the well-indoctrinated crowd.

"The future demands from us something more than a nostalgia for some rose-tinted version of the past that did not really exist in any case," Kerry said. "You're about to graduate into a complex and borderless world" ("...borderless world," aka, the global commune).

In a direct shot at Trump and his supporters, Kerry said, "Many of you were in elementary school when you learned the toughest lesson of all on 9/11.... There are no walls big enough to stop people from anywhere, tens of thousands of miles away, who are determined to take their own lives while they target others." (Only if we continue to import jihadists from the Middle East under illegal migration and the guise of refugee resettlement.)

Meanwhile, at UC Berkeley, HBO comedian and political activist Bill Maher was giving his commencement speech. He highlighted environmental issues and cited his desire to "make a difference" as his inspiration for being liberal, decrying oppression and making jokes about Republicans.

"Never forget that we are lucky to live in a country that has a First Amendment," Maher said. "Liberals should want to own it the way conservatives own the Second." Of course, as Maher championed free speech, he took shots at those with a different political message as if free speech should belong only to leftists of like mind. (It's the message taught in every modern journalism school today.)

"Be confident in your heritage. Be confident in your blackness,"

President Barack Obama told graduates and their families at Howard University's 2016 Commencement Ceremony. As reported by NPR, Janell Ross at *The Washington Post* lauded Obama's call for "empathy and [an] expanded moral imagination" as one of the few surprising and thought-provoking messages that graduates will receive this season. On Twitter, *Slate* writer Jamelle Bouie called the speech "a great mediation on democracy AND a celebration of black life." *(In other words, black lives matter.)*

Coincidentally, the pro-Obama Janell Ross column appeared in *The Washington Post,* which is owned by Amazon CEO Jeff Bezos, who according to a World Net Daily report, just assembled a 20-man team of *Washington Post* journalists with the sole assignment of "digging up dirt on Trump" to be used by Clinton in the November general elections. The leftist anti-American propaganda machine is firing on all cylinders.

At yet another commencement speech at Florida International University, Obama administration National Security adviser Susan Rice made the following statement: "In the halls of power, in the faces of our national security leaders, America is still not fully reflected." Yes, this is the same Susan Rice who knowingly lied to Americans about the events in Benghazi, selling a false narrative about an "organic riot over an obscure anti-Islam YouTube video," while knowing the entire time that it was in fact an anticipated Muslim terrorist strike on a makeshift U.S. Consulate in Benghazi that ended in the death of four Americans.

Rice continued, "Diplomats who can read cultural cues may better navigate the political and social currents of a foreign nation. In sum, leaders from diverse backgrounds can often come up with more creative insights, proffer alternative solutions and thus make better decisions." *(Translation: We need more anti-American representation in government.)*

In case after case, Obama representatives of the anti-American left continued their overt effort to drive deepening divisions down socio-economic, racial, ethnic and ideological lines, encouraging the 2016 graduating class to continue the march to total social division and destruction of a once UNITED states.

This is America circa 2016, where free speech is welcome, as long as what you say is in line with the global socialist agenda. When it is not, you are labeled everything from an *evil right-wing extremist* to a *potential domestic terrorist* for simply standing up for America and the principles and values that once made our country the greatest nation ever known to mankind.

In short, only "black lives matter." If you disagree, you are "racist." Only the gay, lesbian and transgender agenda matters. If you disagree, you are a "homophobe." Only global interests matter. If you disagree, you are an "isolationist." Only democratic socialist principles and values matter. If you disagree, you are a "potential domestic terrorist." Only religious liberty for Islam matters. If you disagree, you are "anti-Islam." Only a woman's right to kill her offspring matters. If you disagree, you are not "pro-life," you are "anti-women." Illegal alien rights matter. If you disagree, you are an "anti-immigrant racist."

As strategically plotted in *Prairie Fire* almost 50 years ago, the so-called "anti-imperialists" busily fundamentally transformed America by "winning over the hearts and minds" of new generations through government-run education and the importing of the global agenda through refugee resettlement and illegal immigration. In the process, the nation was torn into factionalized and easily manipulated voting blocs based upon narrow individual interests. The American electorate was being transformed.

In the end, the democratic socialist cabal represented by Obama, Clinton, Sanders, Kerry, Rice and many more, now including some on the Republican side of the aisle, had become an exclusive club built out of numerous single-interest exclusive clubs. Contrary to propaganda about an "all-inclusive" democratic social experiment which amounts to social engineering at its worst, the democratic socialists (aka anti-imperialists) were co-opting and using every single-issue special-interest group in the country to divide and conquer the United States from within.

If you have read to this point in the book and you are still not convinced that the American people are up against a global initiative (cabal) to end American sovereignty and meld America into a "borderless new world order," or to prevent Donald Trump from keeping any of his politically incorrect campaign promises, one way or another, then consider this…

The international puppet masters known as *The Bilderberg Group* is meeting from June 9 – 12, 2016 in Dresden, Germany. Among the main topics of this annual meeting of the international "who's who" in global power brokers is their panic over the Trump Revolution underway in the west. Consider that famed Bilderberg member Henry Kissinger recently demanded a face-to-face meeting with Trump — and then make note of the USA Attendee list for the 2016 Bilderberg meeting, as posted by *The Bilderberg Group.*[1]

USA PARTICIPANTS AT 2016 BILDERBERG MEETING

This group is meeting June 9 – 12, 2016 in Dresden, Germany:

1. Altman, Roger C., Executive Chairman, *Evercore*
2. Altman, Sam, President, *Y Combinator*
3. Applebaum, Anne, Columnist Washington Post; Director of the Transitions Forum, *Legatum Institute*
4. Burns, William J., President, *Carnegie Endowment for International Peace*
5. Cote, David M., Chairman and CEO, *Honeywell*
6. Engel, Richard, Chief Foreign Correspondent, *NBC News*
7. Ferguson, Jr., Roger W., President and CEO, *TIAA*
8. Ferguson, Niall, Professor of History, *Harvard University*
9. Graham, Lindsey, U.S. Senator (R-SC)
10. Hobson, Mellody, President, *Ariel Investment, LLC*
11. Hoffman, Reid, Co-Founder and Executive Chairman, *LinkedIn*
12. Jacobs, Kenneth M., Chairman and CEO, *Lazard*
13. Johnson, James A., Chairman, *Johnson Capital Partners*
14. Jordan, Jr., Vernon E., Senior Managing Director, *Lazard Frères & Co. LLC*
15. Karp, Alex, CEO, *Palantir Technologies*
16. Kissinger, Henry A., *Chairman, Kissinger Associates, Inc.*
17. Kleinfeld, Klaus, Chairman and CEO, *Alcoa*
18. Kravis, Henry R., Co-Chairman and Co-CEO, *Kohlberg Kravis Roberts & Co.*
19. Kravis, Marie-Josée, Senior Fellow, *Hudson Institute*
20. Levin, Richard, CEO, *Coursera*
21. Malcomson, Scott, Author; President, *Monere Ltd.*
22. McArdle, Megan, Columnist, *Bloomberg View*
23. Micklethwait, John, Editor-in-Chief, *Bloomberg LP*
24. Mundie, Craig J., Principal, *Mundie & Associates*

25. Murray, Charles A., W.H. Brady Scholar, *American Enterprise Institute*
26. Noonan, Peggy, Author, Columnist, *The Wall Street Journal*
27. Petraeus, David H., Chairman, *KKR Global Institute*
28. Rubin, Robert E., Co-Chair, *Council on Foreign Relations*
29. Schmidt, Eric E., Executive Chairman, *Alphabet Inc.*
30. Thiel, Peter A., President, *Thiel Capital*

Take a good close look at the names on that list and ask yourself why you find so many "right-wing" politicos you once trusted, publicly standing with Clinton and Soros against Donald Trump? Then ask yourself — Are you really ready for the Revolution you just started behind the Trump campaign? Are you ready to finish what you started? This is not your country at this moment...

Everything that once made America great was no longer politically correct or socially acceptable. *The silent majority* was overrun by fringe-issue social misfits and anti-American globalists who sought the overt destruction of the United States decades ago, and had enlisted the help of young and unwitting special-interest minority groups.

By 2016, the nation was more divided than at any time in U.S. history and those divisions were at a boiling point. Fueled by leftist community organizers who are adherents to the *Prairie Fire* agenda and who now run our federal government, incidents of school and workplace shootings and public riots were skyrocketing across this once-peaceful nation. Deadly American-on-American attacks were becoming daily headlines in cities from coast to coast.

The simple truth is this: America is FAR from great today—and her decline is no accident. It was intentional. Everything happening in our country today is part of someone's agenda. Nothing is happening on its own, and an ever-increasing number of Americans are rapidly arriving at this realization.

Our Founders warned us to be "forever vigilant" in defense of freedom and liberty. In the words of John Adams, "Our Constitution was made only for a moral and religious people. It is wholly inadequate to the government of any other."

That explains why the "anti-imperialist" progressive left had to assault all of the moral foundations of freedom and liberty. In a very conscious and systematic way, they fundamentally transformed America from its beginnings as a morally conscious Christian nation, wherein everyone was proud to be American without any hyphenated divisions, to a society of morally and ethically bankrupt special-interest voting blocs. These factions were so myopic and so self-centered that they totally lost sight of the principles and values that make greatness even possible.

However, *the people* could never be forever vigilant in defense of freedom and liberty once they had lost all connection to the foundations of freedom and liberty, the Charters of Freedom. A full 240 years after our country won its independence, we were once again dependents of a government which was no longer representative of, or dependent upon *the people*. The foundations of freedom and liberty had been intentionally dismantled and buried like a rotting carcass. Americans were now more interested in freebies than freedom and they no longer cared about the principles that make freedom and prosperity possible.

But something was very different about the 2016 election cycle.

All of the norms of the past were no longer the norm. All of the tricks used to control the outcome of elections before the elections could be held were now failing. The news media, once trusted as the eyes and ears of *the people*, were no longer even thought of as journalists, but rather as mere propagandists of the two major political parties.

As the party powers were visibly losing their grip, they were becoming increasingly panicked over the idea that *the people* had become so fed up with establishment politicians that they were ready to fire everyone in D.C. and start over again, without any regard for old partisan paradigms. The people were angry with everyone in Washington politics. Global news of people tossing out their politicians in Iceland, Greece, Brazil and elsewhere in South America, and rumors of a European Union split over the same poor political leadership now affecting the USA would fuel American anxiety even more.

> *When in the course of human events, it becomes necessary for one people to dissolve the political bands which have connected them with another, and to assume among the powers of the earth, the separate and equal station to which the laws of nature and of nature's God entitle them, a decent respect to the opinions of mankind requires that they should declare the causes which impel them to the separation.* — Declaration of Independence

Once again the time had arrived in America when the course of events made it necessary for the people to dissolve traditional political bands which once connected them. The time had come to cast off the partisan ties that bound them in destruction and rapidly growing universal poverty, and reclaim the constitutional republic that had been systemically violated by everyone in Washington, D.C. for nearly a century.

It no longer mattered to most Americans whether a politician was an anti-American leftist or a do-nothing Republican. Both were now seen as enemies of the people and equally destructive of the republic. The people had lost all faith and confidence in all three branches of their federal government and with good reason.

The public spectacle of D.C. Republicans working hand-in-hand with D.C. Democrats in an overt effort to deny the GOP voters their choice of candidate by any means necessary was the final nail in the coffin of the Republican Party of old. The Republican Party would have to be reborn in 2016, at the hands of *the people*, or it would be left for dead, making room for a new conservative political party that would challenge the destructive political left.

We hold these truths to be self-evident, that all men are created equal, that they are endowed by their Creator with certain inalienable rights, that among these are life, liberty and the pursuit of happiness. That to secure these rights, governments are instituted among men, deriving their just powers from the consent of the governed. That whenever any form of government becomes destructive of these ends, it is the right of the people to alter or to abolish it, and to institute new government, laying its foundation on such principles and organizing its powers in such form, as to them shall seem most likely to affect their safety and happiness. — Declaration of Independence

The American people wanted to matter again. They no longer wanted to feel like strangers in their own country. They wanted America to be great again. They were ready to do whatever it took to retake control of the Republican Party through the primary process wherein 16 candidates were eliminated one by one, until the voters had the person they believed would make America great again. That person is New York-based self-made billionaire Donald Trump.

The final chapter of the Trump Revolution will be written over the coming months, through the July 2016 Republican Convention, the November general election and the new presidential administration taking power in January 2017. The Trump Revolution must be only a beginning of a long-term restoration of our once-great constitutional republic. It may begin with the Trump revolution, which must prevail, but it cannot end there.

The silent majority was no longer willing to remain silent in the face of certain ruin. They were ready to take action and they would do it by peaceful constitutional election processes if they could. This book was written so that all Americans and freedom-loving people around the globe could know why the Trump Revolution is happening, who is behind it, what their intentions are and how determined that movement is to alter the direction of the Republican Party, the federal government and the United States of America.

As we wrap up the final chapter of this book, we have only one recommendation for Donald Trump and all of his followers, current and future: Follow George Washington's example on two counts.

1. After his inauguration in Manhattan as the first President of the newly created United States of America on April 30, 1789, his first act was to walk up Broadway for a service at St. Paul's Church. There, he dropped to his knees and prayed to the Lord above for the strength and guidance to lead the fledgling nation. Trump and his supporters should do the same.

2. Next, the first Chief Executive walked to the New York Society Library and withdrew a book with the stated purpose of learning how to properly govern this new republic and to faithfully execute the supreme law of the land. That book was *The Law of Nations* by Swiss political philosopher Emerich de Vattel, published in 1758. It served as the foundation for everything our Founders created in their original documents, and even today it remains the world's most highly regarded scholarly work on the subject of natural law and natural rights.

Washington so treasured this work that he never returned the book. That fact remained unnoticed until 2010, when a complete inventory of the library's 1789 – 1792 ledger showed it to be missing. When the managers of Washington's Mount Vernon estate were informed that the book was 221 years overdue — and it was not in their collection — they hastened to make amends. In a special ceremony on May 19, 2010, they presented the New York Society Library with a very rare duplicate copy. The library kindly waived the roughly $300,000 in late fees.[2]

As we conclude this book, we recommend to Donald Trump and his supporters, current and future, that they emulate President Washington in these two ways. After dropping to your knees in prayer, asking God almighty to forgive the sins that have allowed our country to arrive at this near-fatal moment in history, and to forgive our failure to be forever moral, ethical and vigilant in defense of the freedom and liberty which were so graciously endowed upon us by our Creator—begin the study of *The Law of Nations* and learn the foundations for the natural rights of any free people, *Natural Law*.[3]

We know of no other way to turn this country around and make it once again one nation, under God, indivisible, with liberty and justice for all. One man, one movement can make all the difference in the world — but only if the people finish what they have started in 2016.

To those of you still thinking about not voting in the 2016 election, voting for Hillary Clinton or Bernie Sanders, both of whom are Marxists, considering a "third party" alternative or writing in the name of anyone already defeated by Trump in the primary process — please return to Chapter I and read this book again. Our country is in desperate circumstances, up against overwhelming odds, fighting a massive global enemy that now operates within the halls of our own government.

If you have read this book and still think any American can afford to sit this election out, for any reason at all, you are not an American. If there are more than a handful of you who are willing to sit it out in the 2016 election cycle, then the future of freedom and liberty for the entire world, is indeed hopeless.

About the Authors

T RUMPED is co-authored by J.B. Williams and Timothy Harrington. Both have served the cause of freedom and liberty for much of their lives, in and out of uniform. They are co-founders of The United States Patriots Union, which encompasses Veteran Defenders of America and The North American Law Center. For decades, both have studied, written about, given countless interviews and drafted many white papers on matters of U.S. constitutional history, national security, military operations and investigations, political crimes and legislative initiatives. Harrington worked on the investigations concerning Hamdania and Haditha, in protection of U.S. Armed Forces on the battlefield. Williams and Harrington issued the first Executive Brief on the events at Benghazi, only 72 hours after the event, and most of that material has since appeared in congressional investigations years later. Williams has published more than 3,000 essays and columns on politics and constitutional history. Both men worked together on Rules of Engagement challenges for active duty military personnel. They collaborated with Billy and Karen Vaughn in the telling of their son's story, *Betrayed: The Shocking True Story of Extortion 17 as Told by a Navy SEAL's Father,* and did much of the investigation into the tragic downing of *Extortion 17* in Afghanistan. They worked to research, model, draft and circulate across the country, state-level legislation in *The Balance of Powers Act.*

On a national level, they have introduced proposed Articles of Impeachment, which identify 48 impeachable acts by the Obama administration, which still continue today. Williams and Harrington have appeared as guests on numerous radio interviews over many years and now oversee a weekly national syndicated radio show TNALC Radio, co-hosted by J.B. Williams and Stephen Pidgeon. Both Williams and Harrington have been researching and writing about the destruction of the USA for over 20 years now. Together, they bring a uniquely qualified view into current events as they connect to the past and the future. This is the first published book by the two authors.…

Notes

CHAPTER II   All Politics is Local

1. Frank R. Kent, *The Great Game of Politics*, (North Stratford, NH: Ayer Co. Publishers, 1923), Preface V.

2. "Baltimore's Kent," Time Magazine cover, (New York, New York: Time Magazine, August 27, 1928), Vol. XII, No. 9. http://content.time.com/time/covers/0,16641,19280827,00.html

3. "Frank Kent," last modified April 28, 2016. Wikipedia, https://en.wikipedia.org/wiki/Frank_Kent

4. Kent, *The Great Game of Politics*, Preface VIII.

5. Ibid., p. 7.

6. Ibid., Chapter 2, p. 6, 8.

7. Ibid., Chapter 2, p. 12.

8. Ibid., Chapter 2, p. 13.

CHAPTER III   Counter-Revolution by Evolution

1. All statements from and reference to *Prairie Fire — The politics of Revolutionary Anti-Imperialism and a Political States of the Weather Underground* are taken directly from the text of an original copy of *Prairie Fire.* Bernardine Dohrn, Billy Ayers, Jeff Jones and

Celia Sojourn, (Red Dragon Print Collective, May 1974, Weather Underground).

2.   Chapter 1, p. 1.

3.   Saul David Alinsky, *Rules for Radicals: a Practical Primer for Realistic Radicals.* (New York: Vintage Books, 1989), http://www.vcn.bc.ca/citizens-handbook/rules.html

4.   References to The Cloward-Piven Strategy are taken from writing by authors Francis Fox Piven and David Cloward, http://www.tandfonline.com/doi/abs/10.1080/07393148.2011.591906

5.   "UN Agenda 21," United Nations Conference on Environment & Development, Rio de Janeiro, Brazil, June 3–14, 1992, https://sustainabledevelopment.un.org/content/documents/Agenda21.pdf

6.   "Global Governance 2025: At a Critical Juncture," http://www.countdown.org/en/documents/global-governance-2025/

7.   Quote by Joseph Stalin borrowed from Gordon State College record of statements by Stalin, http://ptfaculty.gordonstate.edu/jmallory/index_files/page0494.htm

8.   Friedrich Engels and Karl Marx, "The Communist Manifesto," (1848). All references taken from the Congressional Record, Vol. 109, 88th Congress, 1st Session, Appendix pages A1-A2842, Jan. 9-May 7, 1963, Reel 12, http://www.uhuh.com/nwo/communism/comgoals.htm

9.   Friedrich Engels and Karl Marx, "The Communist Manifesto," (1848), cover image, public dopmain: https://en.wikipedia.org/wiki/The_Communist_Manifesto#/media/File:Communist-manifesto.png

10. Reference to Barack Hussein Obama's birth in Kenya to a Kenyan father is taken from Obama's *Harvard Law Review* Biography; reported by numerous sources and cited by *Western Journalism*, (December 9, 2013), http://www.westernjournalism.com/harvard-law-review-bio-obama-born-kenya/

11. Joel B. Pollak, "The Vetting—Exclusive—Obama's Literary Agent in 1991 Booklet, 'Born in Kenya and raised in Indonesia and Hawaii,'" May 17, 2012, http://www.breitbart.com/big-government/2012/05/17/the-vetting-barack-obama-literary-agent-1991-born-in-kenya-raised-indonesia-hawaii/

12. Obama biography image from a promotional booklet produced by Acton & Dystel (1991), http://www.westernjournalism.com/obama-literary-agent-obama-born-in-kenya/

CHAPTER IV   Republican Party on the Brink

1. Mount Vernon Estate of George Washington, http://www.mountvernon. org/digital-encyclopedia/article/presidential-election-of-1789/

2. Statements regarding the story of George Washington and *Vattel's Law of Nations* was widely reported by Reuters, http://www.reuters.com/ article/us-library-washington-idUSTRE64J4EG20100520

CHAPTER V   A Nation on the Brink

1. Quote from J. Edgar Hoover, then Director of the Federal Bureau of Investigation, printed in an August 1956 edition of *Elks Magazine*.

2. Reference to the Cloward-Piven Strategy are taken from the 1966 article in The Nation titled "The Weight of the Poor," written by a pair of radical socialist Columbia University professors, Richard Andrew Cloward and Frances Fox Piven are referenced at Wikipedia, https:// en.wikipedia.org/wiki/Cloward%E2%80%93Piven_strategy and discussed in *Western Journalism,* http://www.westernjournalism.com/ crush-system-cloward-piven-stategy-u-s-border/

3. Writings of Francis Fox Piven and David Cloward, *The Cloward-Piven strategy*, http://www.tandfonline.com/doi/abs/10.1080/07393148.2011.5919 06.8.2011.591906

4. Text quoted from the *Declaration of Independence* from the National Archives, https://www.archives.gov/dc-metro/washington/

CHAPTER VI   The Outsider vs. the Establishment

1. Information concerning the true status of Edward (Ted) Rafael Cruz legal citizenship is documented in the book via illustrations, his Canadian birth certificate from 1970 and his Canadian citizenship renunciation document dated May 2014.

2. Information concerning campaign funding of Levin, Beck and Erickson was taken from reports by Conservative Tree House blog and the Daily Caller — http://dailycaller.com/2016/04/08/ gop-establishment-money-funding-mark-levin-glenn-beck-erick-erickson-to-attack-trump/

CHAPTER VII   All the King's Media

1. Information concerning The Prince by Machiavelli was borrowed from The Constitution Society web site, where the text of the book is posted for public access — http://www.constitution.org/mac/prince00.htm

2. Information concerning WWII propaganda responsible for the election of Adolf Hitler was take from Harvard University archives, http://blogs.harvard.edu/karthik/files/2011/04/HIST-1572-Analysis-of-Nazi-Propaganda-KNarayanaswami.pdf and The U.S. Holocaust Museum, https://www.ushmm.org/research/research-in-collections/search-the-collections/bibliography/nazi-propaganda

3. Additional "pay to play" information provided by The Daily Beast and Politico.

4. Information concerning campaign funding of Levin, Beck and Erickson was taken from reports by Conservative Tree House blog and the Daily Caller, http://dailycaller.com/2016/04/08/gop-establishment-money-funding-mark-levin-glenn-beck-erick-erickson-to-attack-trump/

5. Information on Keep the Promise PAC concerning Glenn Beck and David Barton provided by The Daily Beast and Politico, http://www.thedailybeast.com/articles/2014/01/13/a-right-wing-group-s-400k-purchase-of-mark-levin-s-book-sets-off-a-ruckus.html

6. Information on The Resurgent PAC taken from Conservative Tree House, https://theconservativetreehouse.com/2016/03/30/eric-errickson-website-resurgent-paid-by-pro-cruzanti-trump-our-principles-pac/

7. The "Dump Trump" information comes from Our Principles PAC via USA Today, http://www.usatoday.com/story/news/politics/elections/2016/04/05/outside-super-pacs-republican-delegates-trump-cruz/82662696/

8. The "Dump Trump" PAC information is also noted here — http://www.usatoday.com/story/news/politics/onpolitics/2016/02/21/donald-trump-super-pac-marlene-ricketts/80698232/

9. The list of the top seven "Dump Trump" PACs are reported by Law Newz here — http://lawnewz.com/high-profile/heres-whos-funding-the-anti-trump-movement-and-yes-mostly-conservatives/

10. The new world order reference is based upon Global Governance 2025, UN Agenda 21 and the Council on Foreign Relations North American Union works, reported by Rick Wells in "Heidi Cruz — New World

Order Puppet Exposed," http://rickwells.us/heidi-cruz-globalist-new-world-order-puppet-exposed/, and backed by CFR reports on "Building a North American Community," http://www.cfr.org/canada/building-north-american-community/p8102

11. Ted Cruz ineligibility shown from Canadian government records of his official citizenship papers shown in this book, pp. 58, 60.

CHAPTER VIII Counter-Revolution Meets Revolution

1. Reference to Mitt Romney, Mass-Health and ObamaCare is based on information from http://www.politico.com/story/2014/05/massachusetts-romneycare-health-care-exchange-106362 — and — CATO Institute http://www.cato.org/policy-report/januaryfebruary-2008/lessons-fall-romneycare

2. Reference to Middle Eastern Refugee Resettlement in the USA are based upon UN Reports and the Center for Immigration Studies — http://cis.org/Rush-UN-Role-US-Refugee-Resettlement — and reports by Dr. Rich Swier — http://drrichswier.com/2016/05/22/fraud-waste-and-abuse-in-the-u-s-refugee-resettlement-program/

3. References to Guantanamo Bay terrorist detainees released to battle are borrowed from *Gateway Pundit,* http://www.thegatewaypundit.com/2016/02/confirmed-117-gitmo-detainees-returned-terrorism-far-18-released-detainees/. Also, *The Hill*, http://thehill.com/policy/defense/policy-strategy/234725-intel-community-gitmo-detainees-will-return-to-the-fight

4. Information concerning House investigations into IRS targeting of conservative groups is backed by numerous news reports and efforts to impeach the head of the IRS, http://www.foxnews.com/politics/2016/06/06/irs-releases-list-groups-targeted-in-scandal-3-years-later.html

5. Information on Benghazi was released by North American Law Center only 72 hours after the event, https://www.scribd.com/doc/110758358/Executive-Summary-Brief-Benghazi.

6. Reference to Extortion 17—Afghanistan is based upon information presented *Betrayed* — http://www.forourson.us/order-betrayed.html

7. Reference to the Raven 23 incident is based upon — http://www.supportraven23.com/incident/

8.   Reference to amnesty for illegal aliens under the Reagan adminis-
      tration is backed by NPR, http://www.npr.org/templates/story/story.
      php?storyId=128303672

CHAPTER IX   Cloward-Piven, Alinsky & Democratic Socialism

1.   See previous chapters in this book for more references on the Cloward-
      Piven strategy, Saul Alinsky and UN Agenda 21 Global Governance 2025.

2.   Saul Alinsky's *Rules for Radicals* taken from the book, http://
      www.amazon.com/Rules-Radicals-Practical-Primer-Realistic/
      dp/0679721134

3.   Saul David Alinsky, *Rules for Radicals* book image, public domain,
      https://en.wikipedia.org/wiki/Rules_for_Radicals

4.   Saul David Alinsky on 63rd Street in Woodlawn (1966). Wide public use.

5.   References to Democratic Socialism are all based upon The
      Democratic Socialists of America (DSA), http://www.dsausa.org/
      what_is_democratic_socialism

6.   Quote from former British Prime Minister Margaret Thatcher
      (1925 – 2013), http://www.goodreads.com/quotes/138248-the-problem-
      with-socialism-is-that-you-eventually-run-out

CHAPTER X   No More Democrat Party, No More Racism

1.   Lev (Leon) Trotsky, The Russian Bolshevik Revolution, (Century Co.,
      1921), Wikimedia Commons Public Doman, https://en.wikipedia.org/
      wiki/File:Lev_Trotsky.jpg

2.   Reference to Leon Trotsky's use and intent of term "racist" or "racism"
      is based upon these terms appearing in print for the first time in
      Trotsky's *History of the Russian Revolution*, https://www.marxists.org/
      archive/trotsky/1930/hrr/ — and — is written about in *The Unpopular
      Truth* by Dustin Stanley, http://penetrate.blogspot.com/2010/01/racist-
      word-invented-by-ussrs-leon.html

3.   The Russian to English translation of the statement by Leon Trotsky:
      "Slavophilism, the messianism of backwardness, has based its philosophy
      on the fact that the Russian people and their church are democratic
      through and through, and the official Russian — is a German
      bureaucracy imposed upon Peter. Marx noted in this regard: "For in the

same way the Teutonic jackasses blamed the despotism of Frederick II, and so the French, as though backward slaves were not always in need of civilized slaves to get the necessary training..." This brief comment completely finishes off not only the old philosophy of the Slavophiles, but also the latest revelations of "racists". Multi-language online translation: https://translate.google.com

4. Reference to the *Emancipation Proclamation* and Republican President Lincoln are found in the national archives, https://www.archives.gov/exhibits/featured_documents/emancipation_proclamation/

5. Reference to Democratic Party opposition to the Civil Rights Acts of the 50s and 60s is confirmed in the *Congressional Record* in Roll Call votes and is written about *The National Review* in *The Party of Civil Rights,* http://www.nationalreview.com/articles/300432/party-civil-rights-kevin-d-williamson

6. The Black Lives Matter movement is a $33 million political movement funded primarily by George Soros, http://www.washingtontimes.com/news/2015/jan/14/george-soros-funds-ferguson-protests-hopes-to-spur/ — and led by Obama community organizer Van Jones and *Democratic Underground* — http://www.democraticunderground.com/10027073109

7. Van Jones, Hillary Clinton and Black Lives Matter — http://www.newsbusters.org/blogs/nb/curtis-houck/2015/10/14/van-jones-compares-hillary-beyoncé-proclaims-black-lives-matter-and-Jones was the Green Czar for Obama — http://www.foxnews.com/politics/2009/09/04/radicalization-obamas-green-czar.html

CHAPTER XI   TRUMP: The Unlikely Leader

1. Reference to congressional millionaires and their rate of return on investments, as reported by CNN, http://money.cnn.com/2015/01/12/news/economy/congress-wealth/

2. Gov. Scott Walker held a 47% lead before the beginning of the 2016 GOP primaries, according to a Drudge poll reported by Breitbart, http://www.breitbart.com/big-government/2015/02/02/drudge-primary-scott-walker-crushes-competition-in-online-poll/

3. Cornell University Law School Reference to natural born Citizen appears in Article II of the U.S. Constitution as a requirement for the Oval Office, https://www.law.cornell.edu/constitution/articleii

CHAPTER XII TRUMPED by the People

1. Demographics of the average Trump voter were borrowed from Real Clear Politics survey results, http://www.realclearpolitics.com/articles/2015/09/09/who_are_trumps_supporters.htm

CHAPTER XIII Issues Fueling the Trump Train

1. The top eight issues in the 2016 elections was borrowed from NBC News, http://www.nbcnews.com/politics/2016-election/eight-issues-could-shape-politics-2016-n456671

2. Information on federal unfunded liabilities is based up reports by The Washington Post https://www.washingtonpost.com/news/fact-checker/wp/2013/10/23/does-the-united-states-have-128-trillion-in-unfunded-liabilities/ — and — Forbes http://www.forbes.com/sites/realspin/2014/01/17/you-think-the-deficit-is-bad-federal-unfunded-liabilities-exceed-127-trillion/#1791335110d3

3. U6 unemployment data — http://portalseven.com/employment/unemployment_rate_u6.jsp — and — a comparison between U3 and U6 as reported by CNBC — http://www.cnbc.com/2015/10/02/chart-whats-the-real-unemployment-rate.html.

4. http://inflation.us/americas-most-horrific-jobs-report-in-history/

5. Powerline story on NPR and Harvard Affordable Care Act study result at http://www.powerlineblog.com/archives/2016/03/npr-says-obamacare-is-a-complete-failure.php

CHAPTER XIV Is 2016 The Turning Point?

1. Information concerning the 2016 Bilderberg meeting and the list of attendees was taken directly from the Bilderberg website announcement — http://bilderbergmeetings.org/participants.html

2. Information of George Washington's Mount Vernon Estate replacing a copy of Vattel's *Law of Nations* at the New York library was widely reported at http://www.reuters.com/article/us-library-washington-idUSTRE64J4EG20100520

3. Vattel's *Law of Nations* (book 1), http://www.constitution.org/vattel/vattel_01.htm

Additional notes regarding The Weather Underground

Weather Underground information can be found in declassified FBI documents wherein their leaders were identified as "domestic terrorists." Leaders included Billy Ayers and his wife Bernardine Dohrn.

1. FBI attachment https://www.fbi.gov/news/stories/2004/january/ weather_012904 accumulates research through files and various accounts of their activities and members are well documented.

   a) Students for Democratic Society (SDS): The SDS was a national organization that grew through the 1960s and became more radical in its later years with off-shoots later labeled "home grown terrorist organizations" by national security agencies. People involved with SDS included Don Warden (aka Dr. Khalid Al-Mansour), Bill Ayers, Bernardine Dohrn and Alan Haber, who was part of the Port Huron Manifesto.

   b) Don Warden, UC Berkeley, aka Dr. Khalid Al-Mansour in the U.S.A.: Before converting to Islam and becoming the international front man for the Saudi Royal Family, Warden was the brains behind the Maoist Black Nationalist Movement manifested in the Black Panthers, the Afro-American Association, the Peace & Freedom Party and Students for a Democratic Society (SDS). Warden set out to raise up a Black Nationalist President with the stated platform he put in place in 1966. Malcolm X died due to his involvement with Warden's organizations. Later, Warden groomed and raised Barack Hussein Obama to national prominence and eventually, the White House.

   c) Alan Haber: Haber lives in Ann Arbor, Michigan with his partner Odile Hugonot-Haber. In 1960 he was made the head of SDS while at Ann Arbor, and FBI files mention him as field secretary for that organization. More recently, he has started or tried to start a revival of SDS.

   d) Port Huron Manifesto, Office of Sen. Tom Hayden: Port Huron Statement of the Students for a Democratic Society, 1962.

   e) Bernardine Dohrn: "The Weather Underground" PBS — Bernardine Dohrn and Bill Ayers, PBS, https://en.wikipedia.org/wiki/ Bernardine_Dohrn